Advance Praise for *The Tre...*

Surinder Deol has dwelled deep into Ghalib and has struck a chord with the core of his creativity. He believes in the inner transformation and ecstasy of poetry, and as a translator he has succeeded in unraveling the magical world of Ghalib's charm and his joy and zest for life. Ghalib comes through alive and pulsating in this rendering. He has succeeded where others have failed. His annotations of exotic words and phrases are of added value. Ghalib was never so close to the Western reader as he is now with this work.

Gopi Chand Narang, Ph.D.
Former President, Sahitya Akademi
Author *Ghalib's Thought, Dialectical Poetics & the Indian Mind*

This compendium of Ghalib's verse is a welcome addition to the slim corpus of Ghalib in English translation, not only because it has a sure method, but also because it doesn't sacrifice the essential Ghalib in a foreign tongue, not of the bard's choice.

Satyapal Anand, Ph. D.
Former Professor of English Literature
University of District of Columbia, Washington, D.C.
Author *Sunset Strands*

Surinder Deol's translation skillfully captures the emotional and semantic setting of Ghalib's work with remarkable ease. Translating the untranslatable nuanced poetic text, he has laid out the context beautifully by zeroing in on free verse interpretation and making it accessible to readers who may not have had any exposure to Urdu poetry. Ghalib is trapped in the quagmire of pedantic and listless translations. Surinder brings together his thorough grounding in Eastern poetics and acquaintance with the Western critical idiom to produce a revealing portrait of Ghailb's creative world and his meticulously etched and scintillating translation is destined to blaze a new trail in Ghalib studies.

Shafey Kidwai, Ph.D.
Aligarh Muslim University
Author *Urdu Literature and Journalism: Indian Perspective*

Ghalib is untranslatable, but also irresistible. All translations are doomed to fail, and yet the effort is a well-deserved tribute to his poetic achievement. Here is the latest gallant attempt.

Frances W. Pritchett, Ph.D.
Columbia University, New York, NY
Author *Nets of Awareness: Urdu Poetry and Its Critics*

Surinder Deol has made a brave attempt at this task. Wisely abandoning the possibility of word by word or line by line correspondence between the original and the translation, Surinder has opted instead for poetic integrity in English while trying to convey a broad sense of the mood and emotional and intellectual complexity of the original. These renderings read well in English and will give the uninitiated a wonderful introduction to this major poet of the Indian subcontinent.

Aamir Mufti, Ph.D.
University of California, Los Angeles (UCLA)
Author *Enlightenment in the Colony:*
The Jewish Question and the Crisis of Post-Colonial Culture

The Treasure

For

Vandana —

Develop a free-flowing heart to be a great poet. You have great future ahead of you.

Best wishes.

Surinder Deol

8/30/2014

The Treasure

A Modern Rendition of Ghalib's Lyrical Love Poetry

Surinder Deol

ISBN:	Hardcover	978-1-4828-3398-0
	Softcover	978-1-4828-3397-3
	eBook	978-1-4828-3399-7

To order additional copies of this book, contact
Partridge India
000 800 10062 62
orders.india@partridgepublishing.com

www.partridgepublishing.com/india

Contents

For my father
Sardar Kandhar Singh Shaida
With Love and Gratitude

The paper is finished
but the song to be sung
is not yet finished.
To travel across this ocean
of beautiful words
a new fleet is needed.

Ghalib, I've sung many songs
in my distinctive style.
The rest is for the critics
to turn over in their heads.

Ghalib
I've Sung Many Songs

Foreword

Ghalib towers above scores of Mughal poets like a "victor" as his *nom de plume* suggests. In the realm of oriental poetry, he rubs shoulders with Rumi and Hafiz. His world is too vast and varied to fit into any one category. His ghazals are unique, not only for the intensity of the emotions and thoughts they express, but also for their exquisite charm, and for revealing profound feeling for the beauty of the world. He was endowed with a passionate appreciation of life, yet he deeply questioned the very fundamentals of faith and dogma, and he agonized over the nature of joy and sorrow and the lot of man in the world. His broodings are of the nature of personal discovery and are fresh and profound with a mystic healing touch.

Interest in Ghalib's poetry has steadily grown in recent times. In Ghalib the contemporary mind sees someone who is iconoclastic but who also cherishes the power of human intellect while drawing attention to the need for a spiritual center.

Surinder Deol has dwelled deep into Ghalib and has struck a chord with the core of his creativity. He believes in the inner transformation and ecstasy of poetry, and as a translator he has succeeded in unraveling the magical world of Ghalib's charm and his joy and zest for life. Ghalib comes through alive and pulsating in this rendering. He has succeeded where others have failed. His annotations of exotic words and phrases are of added value. Ghalib was never so close to the Western reader as he is now with this work.

Gopi Chand Narang, Ph.D.
Former President, Sahitya Akademi
Professor Emeritus, Jamia Millia Islamia
Professor Emeritus, Delhi University

Preface

Oscar Wilde once said, "If one cannot enjoy reading a book over and over again, there is no use reading it at all." I must have read *Divan-e-Ghalib* a hundred times, if not more. Each time I find some part of the hidden meaning of a word or phrase that I had missed before, lurking to be discovered in every nook and cranny. I share this experience with Maulana Abul Kalam Azad, the scholar statesman of India, who had said that each time he dipped his bucket into Ghalib's wellspring of meaning, he drew fresh water, the elixir of life.

Ghalib is a category apart in Urdu poetry. His couplets pack a multitude of intertextual references side by side with literal meanings. Even a serious reader might be led astray if he chose the straight path of literality. On the other hand, in some couplets he is so simple and straightforward that to find a meaning well below the surface might not be possible because, except for the literal meaning, there is nothing else. In between these two extremes lie the multitudes of the gems of his couplets woven into the tapestry of his ghazals.

To my mind, the only English poet who can be compared with Ghalib is John Donne, a 17th century poet whom T.S. Eliot gave the sobriquet of a *metaphysical poet.* The reason behind this unsuitable label was not because Donne was of a philosophical bent of mind or a mystic, but exactly like Ghalib, he also connected images, similes and metaphors to create paradigms of unmatched beauty. We know that Ghalib probably never heard of Donne and that he did not have a role model in either Urdu or Persian in metaphor formation to draw inspiration from. In this aspect of his poetry, therefore, he sought guiding light from within and achieved great success.

Do we translate or transcreate a complex poet like Ghalib? Poetry is untranslatable, say those, who have tried their hand on it and failed. So, what is the alternative? Professor V. K. Gokak, a renowned Indian poet of English, wrote in his Preface to one of my collection of poems, "The poet himself has no qualms of conscience if he tries his hand on translation of his own verse, because trans-creation is a legitimate exercise with him: however, if others attempt it there are numerous pitfalls to avoid." Now the pitfalls are many and some just cannot be avoided. One way is to convey the kernel of the *meaning* in the recipient language and garnish only the most *communicable* appurtenances of added trimmings. The other way is to give a literal translation and then write a paragraph or two (or even a whole page) as explanatory add-ins.

Surinder Deol has walked a middle path between these two extremes. Meandering from one to the other (and sometimes back), he traverses the untranslatable terrain but does not avoid it. A limited (but a sure) success is what he achieves, but given the bad translations done by Ghalib pedagogues that we already have, his effort is noteworthy. Let us see his system and how it works. We will cite the paramount couplet of Ghalib's Divan.

Naqsh firyadi hai kis ki shokhi-e tahrir ka
Kaghazi has pairahan har paikar-e tasvir ka

The literal meanings apart, the far-fetched mytho-historical referential context is of a petitioner in a king's court wearing a dress made of *papier-mâché* presenting his petition and appealing for mercy. In this case, the petitioner is the 'man', the 'word written by God', who is wearing the traditional paper dress and presenting his plea. Layers and layers of added meaning are visible. *Shokhi* would point a finger to the beloved who is playful, *paikar-e tasvir,* likewise would present the beloved (God in Sufi terminology), *tahrir* is reminiscent of the fate God has written for each one of His creation – and so on.

Now let us see Surinder's 5-line free verse interpretation.

Words are prayerfully
complaining
about whose playful writing?
Beautiful images are seen
wrapped in paper clothing.

Skillful as the poetic interpreter he is, Surinder has avoided one pitfall by not referring to proto-mythical references and the other by overlooking the literal meaning altogether. Thus, as I said earlier, the kernel has been preserved, but the layers upon layers of subterranean meaning have been ignored.

This, it seems, is not the only trick up Surinder's sleeve; he has many others as well. Let's take one more example.

Shauq har rang raqeeb-e sar-o-saman nikla
Qais tasvir ke parde mein bhi uryan nikla

This is how the couplet is presented in free verse.

Passionate love has dissipated
my fortune.
But it is not me alone.
Look at Majnun in the painting –
trying to cover his nakedness
with rags.

Simple presentation, some might say. I would say superbly condensed– simple, straightforward and easy to understand. Particularly for those who do not know Urdu, its alphabet and its poetry, the full linguistic-cultural import could never be understood unless the translator wrote a full page or more. Let us see what Surinder has avoided by way of ignoring a dozen or more branches growing out of the basic structure. *Shauq* means desire, craving, longing, and yearning. Majnun, a symbol of the proverbial crazy lover pining for his beloved *Laila,* who is presented as *naked* (not nude, but stripped of camouflaging dress), even in a picture of him. The reach of this connotation is that love is such a crazy costume that it deprives its *wearer* of any other dress. It is, indeed, very well abridged. I would say that stripped of all but one of the denotative meanings, this couplet hides much in its thick outer shell but the interpreter has chosen the softest inner edible pulp and presented it to the reader.

The biggest hurdle before any translator who dares to touch Ghalib's verse is the poet's choice in using a particular shade of meaning attached to it. For example, researchers' method of frequency count tells us that Ghalib has used the word *dil* as many as 2,207 times in his Urdu and Persian verse. *Dil* simply means *heart,* but in Urdu poetry in general and in Ghalib in particular, it has a myriad connotative shades of meaning. Over centuries of its use in Persian and Urdu, it has acquired all these shades in a process which linguists call epithetic borrowing. Let us see what this innocuous-looking and innocent-sounding word could mean in Ghalib, depending on its location and conformity to the given syntax. It is heart, the throbbing engine of life, of course, but then, there are desire, aspiration, need, yearning, craving, wish, nostalgia, hunger for/thirst for, wish fulfillment, hope, ambition, passion, hankering after. And the list goes on. So is the word *ishq,* which simply means *love.* I don't know how many times this word has occurred in Ghalib's poetry, but it is safe to say that the count would not be fewer than *dil.* The simple, harmless-looking and sweet sounding word *ishq* would suffice for any one of these feelings: adoration, love, esteem, affection, desire, yearning, want, worship, adulation, idolization, worship, veneration, craze, obsession, madness, lunacy, insanity, folly and more.

Now, in translation, or in transcreation, the word has to be seen in its contextual framework, and, for that matter, the English equivalent has to be found to convey not only the exact sense but also the exact meaning.

A very difficult task, indeed. I would not say that Surinder has taken the easy way out, but only this much. There was no other way at all. If there were one, then it would mean the interpretative, explanatory or revelatory page or two for a single couplet.

This compendium of Ghalib's verse is a welcome addition to the slim corpus of Ghalib in English translation, not only because it has a sure method, but also because it doesn't sacrifice the essential Ghalib in a foreign tongue, not of the bard's choice.

Satyapal Anand, Ph. D.
Former Professor of English Literature
University of District of Columbia, Washington, D.C.

Introduction

> Ghalib (1797-1869) is one of the greatest poets South Asia ever produced and, in my view, the greatest poet of two of its greatest literary languages, Persian and Urdu... If his language had been English, he would long ago have been recognized all over the world as a great poet...
>
> Ralph Russell
> *Ghalib: Life, Letters and Ghazals*

Mirza Asadullah Beg Khan Ghalib lived at a time of great political and cultural transformation in India's history when the established order, the mighty Mughal Empire, was falling apart and the new regime spearheaded by the East India Company was not yet fully in place. Ghalib's entire life of about 72 years was spent in the midst of this turmoil in search of economic security and literary recognition.

The family of Turkish descent lived in Akbarabad, near Agra, where Ghalib was born in 1797. He lost his father when he was 5, forcing him to spend most of his early years with his mother's family where he had no male role model to look up to. He also learned an early lesson on how to live on the generosity of others. There is no reliable account of his early schooling in Agra and therefore we can surmise that he attained proficiency in Urdu and Persian mainly with his own effort.

When Ghalib was 13 he was asked by the family to marry a 12 year old girl from Delhi, where he moved shortly after his marriage and spent the rest of his life in that city. Ghalib compared his marriage to chains being placed on his feet that led him to spend the rest of his life in a virtual lockup. The marriage didn't work out as planned. A tradition bound, religious-minded wife had little to share with her secular husband who enjoyed drinking wine much more than anything else, and spent most of his time with his friends in the men's section of his home. The marriage also failed in building up a family. Seven children were born, both boys and girls, but none survived for more than 15 months. He adopted his wife's nephew, Arif, but he too passed away when he was quite young. Eventually, Ghalib raised two of Arif's children as his own.

Ghalib in his youth was impressive to look at. He was tall with broad shoulders and a round face and a slightly reddish complexion. On why he chose to become a poet and not a soldier, Ghalib once wrote: "I had not the means to ride to war like my ancestors... But the love of poetry which I had brought with me from eternity assailed me and won my soul... The command of armies and the mastery of learning is not for you. Give up the thought of becoming a dervish, and set your face in the path of poetry. Willy-nilly I did so, and launched my ship upon the illusory sea of verse."[1]

By the time he was 16, Ghalib had written numerous ghazals that qualified him for an invitation to poetical recitation events that were at the center of the city's cultural life. More than anything else, he wanted to get access to the Emperor Bahadur Shah Zafar, who was a poet and hosted poetical recitations in his palace. Although Ghalib got invitations for these royal gatherings, he could not get close to the Emperor because the Emperor's tutor, a poet named Zauq, didn't think very high of Ghalib's work. It was only after Zauq passed away that Ghalib gained some influence in the royal court. In fact, he got the job Zauq had held before and was given an assignment to write the history of the Mughal Empire.

Ghalib admitted having had a crush on a dancing girl in his youth and wrote about it in a letter to a friend many years later: "Friend, we Mughal lads are terror; we are the death of those for whom we ourselves would die. Once in my life I was the death of a fair, cruel dancing girl... It is forty

---

1 English translation of excerpts from Ghalib's letters written in Urdu, reproduced in this introduction, is from *Ghalib: Life, Letters and Ghazals* by Ralph Russell and Khurshidul Islam (Oxford University Press, 2003).

years or more since it happened, and although I long ago abandoned such things and left the field once and for all, there are times even now when the memory of her charming way comes back to me, and I shall not forget her death as long as I live."

Ghalib didn't travel much except one long trip that took him to Calcutta in 1827. Calcutta was the seat of the British power in Eastern India and the most modern city in India at that time. Ghalib liked it so much that he stayed there for about two years. Compared to the sorry state of sanitation and infrastructure in Delhi, Ghalib was impressed with wide boulevards, impressive new buildings, and the life style of the new Western rulers. He realized that British had something to offer to the country in terms of new ways of doing things.

The Mutiny of 1857 started when some East India Company soldiers revolted thereby leading to a popular mob reaction against the British rule in which many British officers were killed and several innocent women and children were massacred. The East India Company fought back fiercely and quickly reclaimed the territories they had lost. When the British troops marched into Delhi, there was hardly any resistance. The Emperor was arrested and was exiled to Burma. Ghalib watched with horror when thousands of Muslim men, suspected to be sympathetic to the aspirations of the mutineers, were ordered to be killed by hanging by the wayside trees. He wrote in one of his letters: "Alas! So many of my friends are dead that now if I should die there will be none to weep for me."

Ghalib was afraid of his own well-being and feared that he would be arrested and hanged in the same manner. In order to prove his innocence, he wrote a short book in the form of a diary that contained favorable references to the East India Company and even condemned the tactics of the rebel forces in killing the innocent civilians. But in his private letters to his close friends he expressed his true feelings about the British and their brutal and barbaric actions against the young Muslim men.

Although Ghalib lived in a traditional Muslim society, he did not practice fundamental Islamic beliefs such as five daily prayers, fasting during Ramazan, and pilgrimage to Mecca. His feelings towards the Prophet and his family were more based on personal affection rather than any religious fervor. In his daily life, he subscribed to a modern and secular vision that was totally at odds with society in which he lived. He wrote in one of his letters: "I hold all mankind to be my kin and look upon all men—Muslim, Hindu, Christian—as my brothers, no matter what others may think." He redefined the often-used word *kafir,* traditionally meant to be a derogatory term for Non-Muslims, as the description of a person who was incapable of loving anyone. From this perspective, a Hindu who worshipped and showered his love on his idols was not a *kafir.* He was someone who was practicing his love for God in a different way.

During his last years, Ghalib was not in good health. He had stopped going out. His friends and admirers came to visit him and that was his only contact with the world. Ghalib died in 1869, a frustrated man, thinking that he had not accomplished much in his life.

Ghalib's Poetry

Five Divans[2] of Ghalib's Urdu poetry were published during his life between 1841 and 1863. But the poet had actually initiated compilation of his Divan in 1816 when he was only 19 years old. He showed great intellectual prowess that was remarkable for a young poet writing in his teens.

Ghalib got obsessed at an early age with the idea that the true literary merit of his work consisted in his ability to write in Persian like Bedil, who was his principal inspirational role model. Although Bedil's family came from Afghanistan, he was born in India and he saw the Mughal Empire

2 Divan is a collection of a poet's work, mainly consisting of romantic verse.

reach its zenith under Emperors Shah Jehan and Aurangzeb. Bedil rose to become the great Indian poet who was not only writing in Persian but the one who was also redefining the semantic boundaries of Persian poetry established by great Persian poets like Hafiz, Rumi, Sadi, and Firdausi. Bedil showed his Indian-ness in his poetry by his ample use of stories, images, and poetical forms that were drawn from ancient Vedantic texts written in Sanskrit. This is something that he passed on to Ghalib. But it was not one-way mechanical relationship. While Ghalib borrowed from Bedil to some extent, he also innovated and carved his own path. Ghalib's love for Persian poetry notwithstanding, as we look back, it is solely due to the depth and lyricism of his Urdu ghazals that Ghalib wins the hearts and minds of his readers.

Poetry is the medium that is best suited to illuminating any aspect of life in a manner that elicits deeply felt emotional responses on the part of the reader. Ghalib's poetry is about his inner yearning as a man who was in love with beauty in all forms and about his life experiences, both pleasant and unpleasant, and wave after wave it hits us fairly directly to generate a wide range of feelings. We can be restrained in our reactions, but it is not possible for us to be indifferent.

There are multiple lenses that we can use to look at Ghalib's verse. When we look at the surface, he is a romantic poet par excellence. Most of his poetry is a conversation with his beloved about how much he loves her, how cruelly she treats him, how she is not loyal to him, and how she ignores his pleas and requests. His greatest wish is to die at the doorsteps of his beloved and to be buried in her alley. It is a grand celebration of illicit love, something that the gender segregated society in which he lived forcefully rejected. Contacts between men and women were bound by strict codes of social interaction that made it nearly impossible for any man to talk openly or correspond with a woman outside his own family. This lends a dream-like quality to Ghalib's love couplets and with the use of colorful imagery and suggestive metaphors, the poet takes the reader on a romantic journey that brings joy and suffering in equal measure.

If we dig deeper, Ghalib is much more than a romantic poet. He echoed thoughts common among Sufi mystical poets, but he was not a Sufi. He expressed ideas that came from conflicting philosophical traditions, namely, the concept of *shuniyata* (nonexistence) that is a core belief in Buddhist philosophy and the concept of *maya* that is at the center of Vedantic philosophy. These are the ideas that have deep roots in the Indian culture and its pluralistic traditions. Since these were parts of the evolved and evolving Indian civilization, Ghalib gave voice to them, but he didn't endorse any particular philosophy. He was not a poet with a mission or an agenda. He didn't want to change the world in a certain way. His main concern was human condition, the miseries of daily existence, and to what extent the Creator bore any responsibility for His creation's well-being. Unconditional surrender to and love for God (Sufi approach), Ghalib felt, was incomplete. In a genuine loving relationship, some questioning of the one you love was in order.

Ghalib's work, both in Urdu and Persian, is based on two foundational concepts, namely, enduring love between a man and a woman and beauty in all its human and natural manifestations. True love extends to all beings and it does not recognize artificial boundaries placed around it by religious rituals and social customs. Beauty is the work of a superhuman being, as it exists outside the reach of the destructive power of human hands. A celebration of beauty is therefore a celebration of endless creativity and majesty of its Creator.

In Ghalib's Delhi, pessimism had cast its long shadow on the city that was politically impotent, socially and economically backward, and culturally decadent. Another theme that is prominent in Ghalib's poetry is therefore that of hopelessness, death, defeat and decay. His avowed love of wandering in the wilderness is a manifestation of the desire to flee from the realities of life that had nothing much to offer other than continuous suffering.

Ghalib makes the point that he doesn't fully understand rules that govern existence and nonexistence; he wonders whether there is more in the universe than actually meets the eye. He raises questions: How can we know what we do not know? What is really behind the curtain of illusion, which is reality? What is death? Is there life after death? What happens if one abandons belief in God? Ghalib faced the same problem about which American poet Wallace Stevens wrote in his book *Opus Posthumous* many years later, "After one has abandoned a belief in God, poetry is that essence which takes its place as life's redemption." But there is a problem, as Ghalib realized. The poet has no direct way of knowing reality beyond what the eyes can see or ears can hear.

Ghalib talks of gardens, flowers, changing seasons, clouds, moonlit nights, and the stars. He wants to take his earthly beloved to the garden and see how the flowers react to her presence. He wonders how the trees and bushes try to be of the same height as his beloved. He writes about nightingale's laments, which are symptomatic of separation and love sickness. In a certain way, even the natural world which is a place for joy in one sense is also the place that reminds us of disconnect with our highest aspiration.

Poets often select a language in which they want to write. In most cases, this happens to be their mother tongue. But great poets, whether they select their mother tongue or any other, tend to invent a new language. Ghalib chose to write in Persian first and in Urdu later. But he was writing in Urdu that didn't exist before. He devised a poetic speech by artfully mixing Urdu with Persian words and by crafting idioms and metaphors that were original as well as highly refreshing. This is something that you feel in your gut when you read Ghalib's Urdu prose or poetry.

About This Translation

Ghalib wrote in short lyric form known as ghazal (pronounced *guzzle*), which has deep roots in Persian poetry. Any two rhymed lines of a ghazal (called a couplet) contain an idea that is complete by itself. Ghazal is required to have unity of form because it follows a rhyming scheme AA, BA, CA, DA, EA, and the rest. Each couplet of a ghazal may contain a number of themes or ideas though in practice couplets tend to describe the beloved's beauty and unending frustrations of the lover. You can find thematic unity in a ghazal but that is an exception and not the rule.

Ghazal reached its zenith with the masterly treatment it received at the hands of highly gifted Persian poets like Hafiz. Since Persian was the official language of the Mughal Empire, ghazal style of writing easily found its way into many local Indian languages. Urdu more than any other language was at the forefront of this poetic transformation and there were poets before Ghalib like Mir Taqi Mir who were using this form with great comfort and lyrical flair. The change that we see in Ghalib is the enrichment due to the use of imagistic language and a wide range of topics from purely personal to parochial, historical, cultural, and spiritual.

Given this background, translating Ghalib into another language is a Herculean task. As languages, Urdu and Persian have unique characteristics and a vocabulary that makes it possible for the poet to achieve perfect rhyming. This is something hard to attain in any translation. Some translators of Ghalib have used metrical tools. The result is unsatisfactory in most cases; it doesn't sound well nor does it capture the beauty and sensitivity of thought in the original.

After examining several possibilities, I decided on a novel approach. Each ghazal was given a title, though it is nothing more than a placeholder, or a way to organize the couplets in easily identifiable buckets. In the next step, each couplet was treated as a short poem, complete in itself. Instead of attempting word by word translation I paid attention to capturing the essence and imagery deeply embedded in each couplet while bringing out its organic richness in simple American English without any rhyming scheme. You may call it translation or transcreation, the brilliance of Ghalib's poetry that has enthralled readers for over 150 years has been preserved. But the use of free verse as a poetic form is not *totally free.* There is hidden lyricism in how the lines are arranged and there is soul stirring imagery that retains the magic of the original text. Ezra Pound once told a translator of an ancient Greek poem: "Nobody will give a damn about the meter, if there is flow." Flow is something that the reader should find in this translation.

Those readers, who have had no previous knowledge of Ghalib's poetical work, nor can they read him in the original Urdu script, should find a fairly accurate rendering of the poet's voice in this translation. Other readers, who have read Ghalib's Divan in Urdu should also enjoy this work as there are no difficult words or meanings to decipher and the couplets flow like clear waters of a natural spring, with everything on the surface spotlessly clean, and even the colorful stones at the bottom shine brightly with light reflected from the top.

The Treasure is divided into nine parts. Since these parts are not thematic divisions, their rationale can be questioned. My defense is simple. Ghalib's poetry may be viewed as a huge quantity of premium wine in a large decanter and imagine the reader is sitting in front of this decanter with a drink glass in his or her hand. How do you pour a small quantity for your consumption without a messy spillover? My solution for this problem is to take about 25 ghazals and place them in an easy to handle goblet. As an added benefit, this nine-part segmentation provides space for some personal reflections on selected couplets and ghazals. It is nothing more than a tiny resting place before you move to the next stop on your poetic journey.

Y. B. Yeats wrote an introduction to Rabinderanath Tagore's slim volume of devotional poems called *Gitanjali* that earned Tagore a Nobel in literature in 1913. Yeats talked about *untranslatable delicacies of color* in the work he was commenting on. Blame it on the climate, food or the culture, people from the Indian subcontinent have the habit of thinking in colorful images. These images invariably show up in their writing. In Ghalib's poetry one thing you will find in abundance is the imagery that is not easy to convey in another language. But if I have succeeded in giving you a taste of it, I consider myself extremely fortunate.

Surinder Deol
Potomac, Maryland, USA
June 15, 2014

• •

Consider it to be
a mystical treasure trove
of meaning, Ghalib.
Each word that shows up
in my couplets.

Ghalib
The Fireplace

Ghalib's Preface

Ghalib wrote a preface to the first edition of his Urdu Divan in Persian. The language he used was not only Persian, but also a flowery language with arcane idioms and difficult to understand metaphors. In order to make sense of this preface, one had to spend a lot of time trying to unfold the meaning of the words that he used. Translators have struggled over the years and they have failed to come up with an agreed version.

Given below is an interpretive translation of the original text that provides a flavor of what Ghalib was trying to say:

> *I invite people with good taste and good appetite. There is good news for those who were waiting for one. This has become possible because we have created a new fragrance by burning the rare Indian aloe wood. And remember this wood has not been cut haphazardly. We have used an axe, a knife, and finally a file. No one cuts wood this way. We are trying to cater to the Persian taste as fast as we can. We are not looking for the fire that was extinguished in India. We are not looking for the ashes to provide us the definite proof. This fire can no longer melt the hearts nor it can provide something new to its followers. The fire that we create today is something new and it comes from our talent and we present this most humbly to the Persian Kings Hoshang and Lahrasap. This new fire that has arisen from the straw has the color of the tulip, it's an eye for the fire worshippers, and it is a lamp for the idol worshippers back home. I am a humble human being with only one quality -- I can warm the hearts of my listeners. I have found a spark from the ashes of the fire that I talked about earlier. I sincerely hope that during the next few months the light will reach with the speed of the wings of a fast bird mingled with the fragrance of the aloe wood to the most discerning audience.*

I am a humble writer of a poetical Divan in Urdu that contains a selection of some of my ghazals, but I promise that as soon as I am done with this I shall devote my attention to the Persian Divan and after having done this I will take no pride at all. I hope the literary critics will take a balanced view and would not consider my Urdu Divan as a sign of the wetness of my quill. Nor would they blame me for the adaptations that I had to make.

O Lord, this is a plea of a man who is just coming to existence from non-existence. My name is Asadullah Khan, alias Mirza Nosha and of nom de plume Ghalib, born in Akbarabad and resident of Delhi. It is my desire to be finally buried in Najaf in Persia.

Part One

Words are prayerfully
complaining
about whose playful writing?
Beautiful images are seen
wrapped in paper clothing.

This is the opening couplet of Ghalib's Divan and it captures his view of the badly broken world in which he lived and God's indifference to human condition. The poet faces God and poses a question: Why did you create this universe? What was the purpose? If this is your creation, why do we have so much misery and suffering? Was this creation an act of playfulness or did it have a nobler purpose? People praying and pleading in front of the Creator with paper clothing covering their naked bodies is symbolic of their complete helplessness. In many ways, this sets the stage for Ghalib's struggle to make sense of reality and find a new rationale for our relationship with God.

Ghalib is at his best when he writes about a lover's suffering. *The Heat of Love* [p. 49] is a ghazal that has a consistent and unified theme. It is filled with extreme sadness at the love's unhappy outcome, which the poet readily compares to a raging fire burning down everything. The fire, used as an extended metaphor, exhibits its destructive power at many levels. At the surface, it burns down the physical space in which the poet lived. But the big damage is inside his "emotional" body: the fire has destroyed his longing for union. What greater loss for a lover could be when even the longing for union with the beloved is gone? Such is the intensity of fire that even his sighs, after his physical death, had the heat left in them to burn the feathers of the birds of paradise. The poet is stretching his imagination because no one knows what kind of birds live in the paradise, if at all. His thinking mind is on fire too. He thinks of desert and it is consumed by fire. The mystical interpretation of this ghazal will focus on the poet's reference to paradise and the hint of an afterlife. Given the depth of hurt feelings and the use of fire as a metaphor, we are left wondering whose rejection has caused this massive damage. Is the source earthly or heavenly?

A Seed of Destruction [p. 55] has 12 couplets and three identifiable themes. At the outset, there is a head-on attack on the notion of any rewards in the next life based on one's deeds in this life. The poet confronts the preacher and tells him why his promise of paradise means so little to people who are already in a meditative state or in ecstasy. Somewhere in the middle, the poet celebrates the beauty of his beloved while poking her about her flirtations with the rival. There are some couplets in this ghazal, which can be called self-reflective: the poet expresses the hope of facing the world one day and telling the story of his wounds. He also finds fault with himself about his tendency to self-destruct just like a farmer who unconsciously creates the conditions for lightening to hit his crop. The ghazal ends on a pessimistic note where the poet talks about his extinction (death) but finds some satisfaction in the fact that extinction brings together disparate elements for renewal. There are some exquisite similes and metaphors in this ghazal—garden of paradise is nothing better than a bouquet, blood is like a bead in the beloved's coral rosary, straw is a fiber of a flute, wounds are like clusters of lamps, heart is like Joseph's prison cell, and more.

Pieces of My Liver in a Saltshaker [p. 66] comes out as a meditation on human condition. The first couplet sets the mood that permeates throughout this ghazal. The statement that it is difficult for a man to be a man (or a woman to be a woman) is a philosophical statement. We find some hidden cues that provide partial answers to the puzzle:

suffering that is difficult to be contained, intricacies and failures of loving relationships, and repentance that comes too late. Bringing wounds to the saltshaker is an interesting take on the traditional saying, "To pour salt on someone's wounds."

It Wasn't My Good Fortune [p. 71] excels both in its form and the depth of meaning. The opening couplet is a masterpiece of "hopelessness as a living experience," something that is every lover's fate. There is a never-ending wait for the union with the beloved. And this wait extends with the extension of life, meaning there is no redemption for true love in this life. The tenth couplet captures Ghalib's view of God and the nature of reality. We are unable to see Him because He is unique and He is the only one. Even if there were a smell of duality (meaning there was another like Him) the concept of Oneness would have suffered a hit. The fact is that there is no one like Him. This is consistent with the Koranic view of God.

PAPER CLOTHING

Words are prayerfully
complaining
about whose playful writing?
Beautiful images are seen
wrapped in paper clothing. [3]

Don't ask me how I bear
the sound of hard stones being beaten
in my loneliness.
From morning until evening
I'm digging the river of milk.[4]

Look at the intensity
of my uncontrolled desire.
Even the sword is slipping
out of its sheath and
its breath is skidding out of its casing.

Spread the net of awareness
to unravel the mystery of my words.

---

3 Ghalib refers to the old Persian tradition in which people appeared before the Emperor wearing clothing made of paper to show that they were aggrieved and were bringing a complaint against injustice.

4 This is a reference to the Persian love story of Shirin and Farhad. It is one of Ghalib's favorites. Farhad fell in love with Shirin, the wife or beloved of King Khusrau. The king asked Farhad to dig a canal through the mountain that brought milk to his palace. Just when the task was nearing completion, Farhad was given the false news that Shirin had died. On hearing this news, Farhad killed himself with an axe.

You will end up chasing a bird
no one has ever seen.

Even in this state of bondage
there is a fire under my feet Ghalib.
The chain that binds me
is my own scorched hair.

A GIFT

A diamond as a gift?
To pierce and disfigure my heart?
Rejoice Asad![5]
Your compassionate lover
has arrived.

MAJNUN FACE TO FACE

I saw Majnun face to face
and no one else.[6]
Two lovers wandering.

---

5 Ghalib chose the pseudonym Asad that rhymed well with his given first name but later changed it to Ghalib – a reference to Ali, a cousin of Prophet Mohammad and a revered figure in Shia Islam.

6 The love story of Laila-Majnun is another of Ghalib's favorite stories that originally comes from classical Arabic literature but later it was adapted by Persian poets. Majnun or Qays falls in love with Laila or Layla while they were very young. Due to a tribal family feud, Laila's parents married her to another man. Majnun is overpowered by the madness of love and he spends his life wandering in the desert. Laila is heartbroken and dies. When Majnun discovers this, he comes to Laila's grave and dies.

Wilderness was not so vast.
It was narrow
like an anemic eye.

Lunacy cured
the black spot in my heart
that my yearning
gave it to me.
It made the spot to disappear
just like a cloud of smoke.

I found myself thinking
in a dream
that we met and talked.
When I opened my eyes
there was nothing there.
No loss, no gain.

Here in the school
of broken hearts
I'm taking a lesson of love.
My heart was here with me
and it is mine no more,
not anymore.

My coffin – something at last
to hide my nakedness.
Every dress that I wore while living
showed nakedness of my being.

When told
that his beloved had died
Farhad killed himself
with an axe.

Asad, lovers die for no reason
and they don't need an axe
to die.

A HEART WITH TRACES OF DEEP WOUNDS

You won't return my heart
if it fell by the wayside
and you found it?
My heart was destined
to find its home
in your everlasting embrace.

Love made it possible
for me to enjoy life and
it cured my suffering.
But what to do now
with the agony of love
for which there is no cure?

She charmed my heart
and it betrayed me readily.
What a betrayal!
My sighs were ineffective
and my prayers
they were not answered.

Simplicity and deception.
Obliviousness and cunningness.
She was daring in her amnesia.
Was she setting up a snare?

Buds began to blossom
and I found my heart
with traces of deep wounds.
Never mind the wounds and bleeding.
Glad, something lost
was regained!

I don't know
the condition of my heart,
though one thing
is quite certain.
I couldn't find it
how hard I tried
but you've found it
again and again.

The preacher poured salt
on my wounds
with his admonitions.
Someone should ask him:
What pleasure did you get
by doing this?

THE HEAT OF LOVE

The unseen heat of love
burned my heart.
It burned slowly
just like the smoldering
fire itself.

My heart doesn't long
for union.
Not even her memory remains.
When the fire raged
in my heart
everything was reduced
to ashes.

Giving up everything,
I continue to live
beyond existence.
I've burned feathers
of the birds of paradise
with my fiery breath.

There is no easy way to express
the inflammable nature
of my thinking.
I thought of the desert
in my despair
and it was consumed by fire.

If I had my heart with me,
you would have seen
the landscape of my wounds.
What should I do with the light now
when the inner light has burned down?

Ghalib, it's me and my desire
for sadness.
My poor heart,
seeing how people behave,
it couldn't take it
and lost its spark.

ROSES, SIGHS, AND SMOKE

Passionate love has dissipated
my fortune.
But it is not me alone.
Look at Majnun in the painting –
trying to cover his nakedness
with rags.

The wound that you inflicted
didn't appreciate
the strength of my heart.
Your arrow came out of my chest
broken into little pieces.

The smell of roses,
sighs of aching hearts.
And the smoke of the lamps.
Whoever came out of your parlor
was a bundle of nerves.

My heart was ambrosial,
fit for a feast of the gods.
My friends had to simply
dig their teeth into it.

If you are a novice
in the art of extinction
be ready to hit a snag.
Trying extinction
when you're already extinct!

Ghalib, the cries of my heart
grew louder and louder.

There wasn't even a teardrop,
but it became a deluge
in the end.

A CORPSE WITHOUT A COFFIN

If a threat can kill you
then you are unfit
for the battle.
Sign up for love only
if you're a world-class
hard nut!

I was paranoid about death
and was afraid to die.
My complexion
had turned pale
before I died.

I kept myself busy
compiling volumes
on the art of love,
though my thoughts
were scattered and fragmented

Between my heart and my liver[7]
there is a river of blood.
It had the color of flowers

---

7 Like other Urdu poets, Ghalib often uses words like heart and liver interchangeably. In some places, liver is used to denote courage, pride, or self-esteem distinct from heart which is the center of love or compassion.

before I fell a victim
to the madness of love.

The strife over my love's anguish
it seems will never end.
My heart is long gone
but the pain persists.

My friends failed to diagnose
my madness.
While in prison
I was actually wandering
in the wilderness.

This corpse without a coffin
is that of a wounded lover
named Asad.
May God bless his soul!
A stranger who lived
as a free man.

IN THE GARDEN

I liked her holding a rosary
in the palm of her hand.
But those were actually
one hundred hearts
of her lovers.

Pessimism brightens my day
and makes life easier for me.
But I do have

a strange way of unraveling
the mysteries of life.

A stroll in the garden
revealed a secret
about her murderous ways.
She liked blood-colored flowers
while thinking of pierced hearts.

THE BREATH OF JESUS

The mark of loyalty
gave no satisfaction
to anyone in this world.
The word is empty from within,
devoid of any meaning.

The shine of an emerald
can make a snake blind.
But your green looks can't subdue
your rebellious tresses.

I wanted to free myself
from the sorrows of love.
But my tormentor
was not ready to let me die.

The heart is a passage for sins,
of loving wine and drinking.
The path of abstinence is an ideal.
But it is not made for me.

You didn't promise to come
and as such there was no false hope.
But my ears were simply not ready
to hear the bad news.

Is there anyone willing to listen
to the tale of my bad kismet?[8]
I wanted to die.
But even that didn't happen.

Just one movement of your lips
killed Ghalib.
Even the breath of Jesus
could not have saved him.

A SEED OF DESTRUCTION

Zealot praised the garden of Rizvan[9]
as the only real thing.
But when you are in ecstasy,
it is no more than a bouquet
inside a dome.

What can I say
of the effort of her piercing
eyelashes?
They have drawn my blood

[8] Some Persian and Urdu words, which are commonly used in English, have not been translated. They include *kismet* (fate), *Saqi* (cup-bearer in a tavern), *kafir* (non-believer or idol-worshipper).

[9] Gatekeeper of paradise and keeper of its gardens.

for the red stones
of her rosary.

My sighs failed to show
reverence to my murderer.
The straw that I held in my teeth
became the fiber of a flute.

I will show you the spectacle,
if time permitted.
Every wound in my heart
makes a cluster of lamps
to shine.

When you appeared
in the house of mirrors,
it changed the place.
Sunrays covered the earth
and filled it with freshly minted
dewdrops.

Within me
there is a seed of destruction
and it invites disasters.
Just like a peasant's granary
is prone to lightening.

My home is green
with weed and grass.
Rejoice wilderness!
My grass-cutter
is not going to be pleased.

My silence hides
thousand storms
of unrealized hopes.
I am a burned-out lamp
without a voice
at the grave of a stranger.

She is gone
but her image lives
in my imagination.
My heart is like Joseph's prison[10]
brightened by his presence.

Did you sleep today
by the side of my rival
by any chance?
I saw you in a dream
and found
a mischievous smile
on your face.

I can't guess
whose blood turned into water.
I saw your eyelashes laced with tears
and it was a Doomsday.

Ghalib, the path of extinction
is within my sight.
It is a thread that binds
unsettled elements
floating around
in this universe.

---

10 Joseph, son of Jacob, from the Book of Genesis.

A DISGUSTING FEELING

Though I am tired
my desire to wander
has not diminished.
On the fast moving waves
you can't miss one thing –
my footprints.

I loved my garden.
But the spirit of that love is gone.
The smell of flowers
disgusts me.

PRAYING FOR LIGHTENING

I promised to love you.
And from head to toe
I became love.
I prayed for lightening.
So why did I cry
when it actually hit me?

Saqi be fair and serve
matching everyone's thirst.
If you are the river of wine,
then I'm the stretch
of its banks.

DRINK GLASSES ARE DANCING

You are not alone
in not knowing the mystery.
The veil you see
hides a melody
that we do not understand.

The color of your skin
is pale and weak.
Is this how the morning arrives?
Or is this symbolic
of your playful flirting
and romantic overtures?

When you look at the stranger
with annoyance,
your long eyelashes
raised in fury
pierce my heart.

I should hold on to my grief
calmly and carefully
lest it destroys me
with the immensity
of its expression.

Drink glasses are dancing
as if lavishly wined and dined.
The lounge seems to be bouncing
over the head of a tosser and a catcher.

My heart wants to untie
the knot of grief

but not the nails.
They owe a debt,
they should remember,
to the half-opened knot.

When separation from you
devastated Asad,
a treasure trove of secrets
of his love
was destroyed too.

A DOORLESS DOOR TO HEAVEN

In the presence of the Emperor[11]
couplets found an outlet.
Let this door stay open.
These verses are as precious
as pearls.

The night came.
And there was a display
of brightly lit stars
and a door was opened
to the house of idols.

I am mad but I'm not ready
to be deceived by my friends.
They hide daggers
up their sleeves
and keep a knife in their hands.

---

11 Bahadur Shah Zafar, the last Mughal Emperor and Ghalib's patron.

She is still a mystery to me.
I do not understand her talk
or her secrets.
But isn't it enough
that she has opened up to me?

Thinking of her beauty
did a lot of good to me.
A door opened from my grave
to the vistas of paradise.

Her face was covered
and I missed a spectacle.
Not only the hair,
even the face-covering
was breathtaking.

She invited me
but she posed
as if she never did ask.
I did bring my bedding with me
and it took me no time
to unroll it.

Why is the night so dreadful?
The stars have shut their eyes
with fear.
When something strange happens,
I look the other way.

How can I find happiness
in this miserable state?

The mailman brings letters[12]
from my home
that are unsealed.

I am a follower
of someone who makes things
happen for me.
Ghalib has to go through
a doorless door
to arrive at Heaven!

FRESH BLOOD POURING DRIP BY DRIP

Last night
my heart was on fire.
So much so, it melted the clouds.
The whirling vortex was nothing
but a leaping flame.

I can't come
because it's raining.
That's what she told me.
My pillow was wet with my tears.
It seemed like a flood.

She was obsessed
adorning her hair with pearls.
Because my eyes were flooded
with tears,
I didn't see anything.

12 A common belief at that time that unsealed letters brought bad news.

In your waterway
there were flowers.
In my eyes
there were tears of blood.

My head hurt
due to sleeplessness.
And there she was
sleeping on her silken pillow.

My breath was lighting candles
and I was in a state of rapture.
She was enjoying
the splendor of flowers
in the company of her friends.

For her there was a storm
of colored waves
from floor to the heaven.
For me there was jealousy
and heart burn
from earth to the sky.

Without much effort
fresh blood started to pour
drip by drip.
My heart was foolishly appreciative
of the great work done by my nails.

A BLACK RUE SEED

My sighs last night
were like a black rue seed[13]
thrown into the fire.
It was a good omen
for my rival[14]
who enjoyed your company.

My heart danced with joy
when the flood destroyed everything.
Before the abode of love was lost,
water made a melodious
reed sound.

There is merit in humility and
the simplicity that comes with it.
Worries fly away
when you rest your head
on a bed of mink.

My devotion was of no help
though every particle
in the universe
waited for the magic
to occur.

Why are you impervious today
to the state of your captives?

---

13 A black rue seed when thrown into fire is believed to be a protection against evil.

14 Rival in Ghalib's poetry is the false lover who is trying to steal his beloved and his happiness. As an abstraction, rival is the force that stands in the way of having something that we cherish in our life.

Until yesterday,
your heart was the model
of benevolence and fidelity.

Do you remember the time
when your snare
caught everything?
And you looked
at your prey
with dreamless and
sleepless eyes!

I restrained Ghalib last night
lest all might have seen
the aftermath.
His tears could have turned
the sky
into a foam-like flood.

A CITY OF MOURNFUL ASPIRATIONS

I had to account for
every drop of my blood.
Only your eyelashes
could have pierced me.

It is I and the city
of mournful aspirations.
Every little piece
of the broken mirror
reflected myriad images.

Take my corpse and
drag it into her alley.
I really wanted to die
on the path
that she frequented.

Don't ask me
about the intensity
of the waves of the mirages
in the desert.
Every particle
had the shine
of an edge
of a sharp sword.

Little did I know
about the sorrows
of unrequited desires
and all that.
When I regained my senses
it was all about
making a living.

PIECES OF MY LIVER IN A SALTSHAKER

It is difficult
for every little thing
to be easy.
It is difficult for a man
to be just a man.

My incessant crying
is destroying my home.
The walls and doors
are revealing my days
in the wilderness.

Pardon me
for the intensity of my desire
that all this time
I tried to reach you
and then wondered
about it.

When you display
your beauty
you really mean to be seen.
Even the lines in the mirror
want to be
your eyelashes.

Don't ask me
about the joy of being taken
to the killing field.
A naked sword,
a crescent moon.
What a way
to celebrate Eid!

I took to my grave
my longing for happiness.
Your presence
and the one hundred ways
to rejoice.

My heart is wounded
and the pieces of my liver –
how do they taste
after they are thrown
into the saltshaker.

She promised to kill
no one after my slaying.
Alas!
What a repentance
of the repentant.

Ghalib, I do pity
the condition
of a foot long costume.[15]
Its fate was sealed
when it became
a lovers' collar.

MAJNUN'S HOME IN THE DESERT

Waiting for Saqi
last night
was like the Day of Resurrection.[16]
Even the wine
was tired waiting
and there was yawning.

---

15 When a lover tears his collar, he demonstrates his grief and frustration thereby exposing his naked chest and heart underneath for the tormenting beloved to see.

16 Or the Day of Judgment. The day when the dead assemble to hear God's judgment.

When I put my foot
into the frenzy
I discovered
a world of possibilities.
The thread
that binds this world
and the next is wilderness.

Who stopped Laila
from frenzied walking?
Majnun's home
was an ocean of sand
without any doors.

Cheap make-up is awkward.
Hands in debt to henna
and the face pawned
to the white powder.

The sighs of my heart
were like the pages
of thin paper
that breeze carried away.
The sighs were my unbound verse
and they were lost forever.

A FAMINE OF LOVE

Friends can't be of much help
during the days of suffering.
By the time wounds heal,

won't the nails be
long once again?

The way you ignore me,
it really hurts.
I'm telling you
the state of my heart
and you say, "What?"

If the preacher comes,
my heart and eyes
will be on his pathway.
But will anyone explain to me,
what could he
possibly explain to me?

I go to her with sword
in one hand
and shroud
in the other.
I wonder
what excuse will she offer
for not killing me?

Zealot imprisoned me.
Not a big deal!
But will I give up
this madness of love
for his sake?

As serfs of your tresses,
we are not running away
from the chains.
If we are prisoners of love,

how could we be afraid
of the jailhouse?

Asad, in my neighborhood,
there is a famine of love,
my staple food.
Granted that I have to live in Dilli[17],
then what exactly
am I going to eat?

IT WASN'T MY GOOD FORTUNE

It wasn't my good fortune
to realize oneness
with my beloved.
Even if I had lived longer,
I would have suffered
the same wait.

If I lived on your promise,
please understand,
I didn't believe it.
Had I believed it,
I would have died
joyously.

Your delicate being
made your commitments
tenuous.

---

17 Colloquial expression for Delhi.

If your promises were firm,
even you couldn't break them.

My heart knows the hurt
of your half-drawn arrows.
There had been no pinch
if the arrow
had gone past my liver.

What good is friendship
if friends became evangelists?
I wish someone
was a pain-reliever
and a comforter.

The blood
from the veins of the stone
was not stopped.
What I thought was sadness
was actually a spark.

Sorrow is a killer
with no escape --
the price of having a heart.
If there were no miseries of love,
there would have been worries
about mundane things of life.

I need someone to share
the horrors
of the night of separation.
Death was normal
if that happened just once,
and no more.

Why didn't I drown myself
in a river
to avoid notoriety?
It would have saved a coffin,
a grave and a stone engraving.

No one can see Him
because He is unlike
anything else.
If there was another,
we would have certainly known.

Ghalib, your elucidation
of mystical matters
was divinely inspired.
Imagine being a sage
if you had stopped boozing!

THE VAGABOND WIND

Greed drives us
to accomplish much
before we die.
But if there was no death,
life wouldn't be
as much fun.

What do you really gain
by showing your ignorance
on purpose?
You understand what I say
and yet you seductively ask,

"What? What?"

I see
how you pay attention
to the other,
but never complain.
Take my protest in stride
and not make any fuss
about it.

I want your
undivided attention
and not indifference.
How long would you really take
to test my patience?

Lustful desire of the other
is like dried stalk of grain.
It would burn in one breath
because it is not true love.

Each breath
is a wave of ecstatic rapture.
Saqi's indifference?
I have no complaint.

If I didn't like the perfume
she was wearing,
then why would I agonize about
the vagabond wind?

Each drop of water sings,
"I'm the ocean."
I belong to Him

the same way,
no doubt.

What are you afraid of?
Look at me,
I give you my word.
There is no blood money
for the people you kill
with your glances.

Listen to me,
O Pillager, of the object of true love.
How do you value
the sound
of a broken heart?

I've never claimed
patience
to be my strength.
Patience and love
do not belong together.

The killer's promise
to kill me
is taxing my patience.
This suspense
and not the fear of dying
is sapping my strength.

Ghalib, everything about her
is heart wrecking.
The way she speaks.
The way she looks.
And the way she flirts.

GHALIB WILL BE BLOWN INTO PIECES

If there was
no one worthy of anger
and punishment like me,
then it is understandable
why no one like me
was ever created?

Even in bondage,
I'm free and demanding.
I would turn back
if I find the door to Kaaba[18]
shut.

We accept the claims
of your Omnipotence.
Looking into the mirror
we see ourselves.
Nothing else.
Maybe you're deep down
within us.

I'm frail and feeble
like your eyes.
Compliment aside,
I'm your patient.
What's wrong
if I didn't get well?

---

18 Kaaba in Mecca, Saudi Arabia, is the most sacred site in Islam. During Hajj pilgrimage, pilgrims walk seven times around the Kaaba in a counter-clockwise direction.

A sigh that got stuck
on my lips became the scar
of my heart.
Drop that didn't merge
into the ocean became
food for the desert.

My suffering
is something no one else
has ever received.
The commotion in my life
didn't happen to anyone,
anywhere.

The blood didn't drip
from the root of hair
after listening to my tale of woe.
It sounded like the tale of Hamzah[19],
not my personal story.

If we can't see river
in a drop of water
and whole in the part,
then it's a child's game
and not like gaining
any deep insight.

Today's headline news --
poor Ghalib
will be blown into pieces.
I expected a big spectacle,
but nothing much happened.

---

19 A legendary storyteller.

A MAD RUNNER

Asad,
I'm running away in madness,
without head or feet,
as if chased by a deer
and the animal's eyelids
are digging into my back

A SHORT LETTER

Lacking in piety
and I'm not reaching out to Him
as I should.
My piety is laced
with hundreds of colors –
each one a particular sin.

A display of beauty
should not bring
the disgrace of infidelity.
Why can't people
just lower their eyes
and not see her?

Pour the white sparkles
of your beauty
into the sun-shaped
begging bowl
for me to light
my darkened quarters.

You thought
I was guilt-free
and you didn't kill me.
But you killed
our friendship.
I wanted death
at your hands.

My tongue was unable
to say thanks
and so I was quiet.
This erased
the need for my complaint
of helplessness.

The oneness of my breath
and the scent of flowers
is something special.
When the flowers bloom,
they make my melodies
more colorful.

Your friends taunt me
for loving you
despite your infidelity.
So many mouths,
so many catcalls!
Infinite. Infinite.

Do not prolong
your letter Ghalib!
Just keep it short.
My desire to share
the story of separation
will remain unfulfilled.

Part Two

Desire complains
about the narrowness
of my heart.
Like a tumultuous ocean
engrossed in a pearl.

This couplet from *A Tumultuous Ocean Engrossed In A Pearl* [p. 88] is reminiscent of a situation that lovers face in trying to manage a flood of desires. They seek union because they can't live in separation. If nothing else were possible, they would like to steal a glimpse of the beloved from a distance. These desires form an unending chain. They multiply with each passing day. But heart, which is the emotional center of the human body, is unable to carry this load. The result is a metaphorical ocean trying to contain itself inside a pearl. The pearl-like heart eventually breaks down – a situation that Ghalib alludes to in several other couplets. When heart falls apart, it turns itself into a stream of blood that drips through the lover's eyes.

Memory is the richest source of great romantic poetry. Time that lovers spend together and even the agony of separation—these things are not easily forgotten. With the passage of time, they find words to gain freedom, an escape that turns a personal memory into a shared one. In *I Remembered* [p. 97] the poet is reconstructing a lover's deeply emotional moments from his recent past using recollective memory. Everything remembered comes back as an image burdened with feelings of loss – having suffered a heartbreaking separation from the beloved. Any thought of the beloved's absence brings up tears to the lover's eyes. His life is like an endless Doomsday, but the memory of separation from the beloved gives more pain than Doomsday's tumultuous confusion. This agony conjures a thought that lovers generally don't entertain: "Why did I fall in love with you? I could have lived my life without you, without this misery…" In the sheer frenzy of love, the lover is even knocking at the doors of heaven and picking up a fight with the heavenly gatekeeper in an effort to find his beloved's abode there. The ghazal ends with a reflective note on Majnun's love story. Because Majnun had embraced madness after his forced separation from his beloved Laila, stones by the wayward kids often hit him. Ghalib metaphorically enters the body of one of those kids but because he remembers his own failed love that led him to some form of madness, his hand freezes in the air thinking that one day he might suffer the same fate. A stone thrown at Majnun would be the stone thrown at his own head. An unbreakable thread binds lovers in their madness: unconditional love for the beloved. American poet Adrienne Rich translated this couplet in its naked simplicity:

I too, like other boys,
Once picked up a stone to cast
at the crazy lover Majnun;
some foreboding stayed my hand.

In *The Wisdom of Six Directions* [p. 105] the poet starts and ends with a complaint against his own heart. "My heart is not the same of which once I was so proud of." There are two mystical couplets that need further explanation. The fourth couplet powerfully employs the mirror metaphor, which in Ghalib's poetry is true and objective representation of reality. Compare this with our own seeing. We look upon reality through the lenses of our own biases and interpretations. As humans we are thus incapable of inventing a device that shows them in their true colors of ugliness such as greed, selfishness, and egoism, the mirror has to be the work of a supra-human entity, a magician. Wherever we look, there are mirror doors, leading us into the house of mirrors. The six directions (or senses) are multiple entry points. We can choose whatever door gives us comfort. But choose we must. Once we are inside, there is unity of perception – nothing is perfect, nothing is flawed. Images appear as the true representation of who we really are. We can't run away from our own reality. This couplet is essentially an invitation for self-discovery. The fifth couplet is about beauty's revelation. As the beloved wears a veil, the lover can't see her face. But his passion is so strong that he has loosened the ribbons that keep the veil in its place and as a result the beauty is revealed. Here comes the challenge. Where can the lover find the eyes to see the beauty in its splendor and magnificence? So in the end, eyes are the only obstacle or barrier between the lover and the beloved. A mystical interpretation points toward the inability of the human eye to see the Beloved. Even if the veil is dropped, our yearning would remain unfulfilled because this particular union is not possible with a body of flesh and bones and our vision unfortunately is limited to seeing only the worldly and mundane.

The Colors of Reality [p. 113] is an amalgam of observations about life and objective reality that exist beyond our senses. A drop falls into the river and becomes the river. This is the goal of every lover who seeks oneness with the beloved. But human relationships are complex. The journey is rough and the surface is rugged. Things fall apart when they give the appearance of moving in the right direction. The chord can break suddenly without any reason, showing unpredictability of human outcomes. Lovers always try their best. If they can't win the love and kindness of the beloved, they pray for beloved's cruelty to persist. Apparently, her torture is better than her indifference. The last couplet of this ghazal is a celebration of spring when the spring is in full bloom and much more. The poet mentions that spring is the best time to sharpen one's vision because there is so much natural beauty to be seen. How can we train our eyes to see more and see more deeply? This question leads us to a mystical inquiry about the nature of being and the need for blending-in with the environment that surrounds us.

ISSUES NOT RESOLVED

The pain of the night of separation
has become a spot on the moon
though my lips are sealed.
Would she not see it
when she looks at the moon?

During the night of separation
my anger may turn itself into water.
But would it not make
the moonlight to reflect and
shine on water?

Kissing her feet while she sleeps
is a beautiful thought.
But since she is a kafir,
I'm afraid, my idol worship
would upset her.

I never doubted the faithfulness
of my heart but there was something
that I didn't know --
it would fail its first test.
She got it at the very first sight
and it was gone for good.

You live inside every human heart
and if You are pleased,

the whole world
is kind to me.

If your angry glance
continues to crush my passionate love,
my blood will become dry like a straw
and then disappear from the veins.

Don't take me to the garden.
Looking at my condition,
every fresh rose in the garden
will have blood dripping
through its eyes.

Our issues will not be resolved
even on the Day of Judgment,
though I've lived with the hope
that it would all be settled there.

What's the gain?
Think about it, Asad.
You too are a wise person.
In trying to befriend a fool,
you will only create a problem
for yourself.

NO MELODY TODAY

My pain refuses to owe
any debt to the medicine.
I didn't consume one dose.
Nothing gained, nothing lost.

Why are you gathering
all my rivals?
Do you want a spectacle
or you want to hear my laments?

Where can I go to try my luck
when you don't want to test
your dagger throwing skills
at me?

Your honey-coated lips
made my rival take your earful
without any bad taste
in his mouth.

There is a word
about your impending visit.
Just today,
I don't even have
a rag in my home.

Namrud[20]
called himself a God.
What for?
I am for selfless devotion.
What for?

He gave me life.
I gave it back to Him.
Dying it seems
didn't repay the debt.

[20] Namrud, the King of Babylonia, who had ordered killing of all newly born children to save his kingdom.

My wound was subdued
but the flow of blood
didn't end.
The work stopped
and didn't begin again.

Is this a robbery
or a way of teasing me?
She took my heart
and walked away.

Recite something.
People are talking
under their breath.
Sadly, today no melody
gushes from Ghalib's heart.

A TUMULTUOUS OCEAN ENGROSSED IN A PEARL

Desire complains
about the narrowness
of my heart.
Like a tumultuous ocean
engrossed in a pearl.

My letter I know
will remain
unanswered.
But my love
drives me to write,
again and again.

What is spring?
Henna
on the autumn's feet.
Fleeting joy
is the source of
lasting sadness.

Don't ask me
to take a walk
in the garden.
I can't withstand
the sound of laughter
in the sadness
of my separation.

My longing for beauty
is my timeless yearning.
The root of every hair
on my body sees you.

In her one flirtatious move
she got my heart.
When beauty demands,
brain simply freezes.

The flow of my tears
is not proportional
to the anguish in my heart.
A river is
continuously flowing
behind the barricades
of my eyes.

I look skyward
and think of her, Asad.
The same way
I look at the sky
and think of Him.

A STRING OF PEARLS

Because the drop of wine
lost its breath
in a moment of surprise
as it touched her lips,
the goblet was completely filled
with a string of pearls.

Look at the destruction
of her trust in my love for her.
When someone else sighed,
she got upset with me.

A HEART TIED TO EVERY PARTICLE OF SAND

Whenever
she readied her carrier
for travel,
the intensity of my desire
tied a heart
to every particle of sand.

Those who could see,
saw the beauty's trifling way.
The green spots on her mirror
fluttered like parrots.

It is like despair and hope
going for a deadly fight
as I go to see her.
My low esteem casts a spell
on my beggar heart.

Ghalib, I couldn't contain my thirst
for the expression of my love,
though I made an effort
to keep the river behind
the barricades.

THREAD AND NAILS

I came back
from your party
thirsty and parched.
If I had given up drinking,
what happened to Saqi?

A single arrow
pierced my heart
as well as my liver.
In one move she got
my heart
and my liver.

In my current state
of desperation
nothing works Ghalib.
When the thread had no knots,
nails were there
to do the job.

THE DOORKEEPER

My house
would have been a ruin
even if I had not cried
like a lunatic.
If my tears had not become
an ocean,
there would have been
a desert.

Why complain
about the narrowing
of my heart?
If it were not hopelessly sad,
it would have been troubled
for sure.

A lifetime of abstinence
is enough
to persuade the guard
at the gates of heaven.
I wish she had over here
an equally sympathetic
doorkeeper!

HEAD DETACHED FROM THE BODY

When there was nothing,
there was God.
Even in the midst of nothingness
God was still there.
My being has really sunk me.
Who would have missed anything
without me?

When miseries of life hit me
I was not sorry
that my head was cut off.
If it had not detached
from the body
it would have been resting
on my shoulders.

Ghalib died a long time ago,
but his memory is still fresh.
He spent his life asking:
what would have happened
if this happened,
or that happened?

FLOWERS AND THE NIGHTINGALE

Every bit of land
in this garden
has been rightly used.
Even the walkway

with tulips
is like a wick of flaming red.

Who has the power
to bear the frenzy
of awareness without a drink?
My helpless state
is rushing me
toward a shot glass
to get high.

The nightingale sings
a melancholy song
and flowers laugh at her.
Love is nothing
but the loss of one's
mental poise.

The intoxication
of the poetic thoughts
is nothing new for me.
Like a mature opium eater
I am the smoke
around the lamp of ideas.

I freed myself
from the jailhouse of love
one hundred times.
But what can I do
when my heart is the enemy
of my freedom?

When there is no blood
in the heart

what you see is a wave
of dust storm.
It is like looking
at the empty shelves
and asking
where's the wine.

When flowers bloom
the heart is filled with joy.
Who pays attention
to the clouds of spring
or the noise
inside the tavern?

AN EXTRACT OF STUNNED EYES

Looking at the wrinkles
on my forehead,
she understood
my hidden sorrow.
The scribble of the address
on the envelope revealed
what was written
in the letter.

The lines in the mirror
are not straight
though I have polished it
many times.
I have been tearing up
my collar
since the day

I understood
why it was there.

Please do not ask me
the reason
why I got arrested.
My heart got narrower
and narrower
until the time
it became a prison.

I didn't want her to go
for a walk on a warm day.
Sweat drops on her face
would have resembled
the extract of stunned eyes.

I knew she would be mad
because I showed weakness.
It is like feeling the pulse
of a straw whose destiny
is to catch fire and burn.

The journey of love
has been long and tiring.
Every step of the way
I used my own shadow
for a restful night of sleep.

I avoided arrows
of her eyelashes
until the time of my death.
But running away
from my destiny

was not as easy
as I thought.

Asad,
why did I give my heart away
without checking her intent?
My mistake --
she turned out to be a kafir
who I thought was a Muslim.[21]

I REMEMBERED

Once again,
I remembered my eyes
dipped in tears.
My heart and liver
crying with longing
and complaining.

As soon as I was finished
with the Doomsday
when I remembered the time
of your travel and parting.

The simplicity of my desire.
Alas!
I remembered the one
with the magical eyes.

---

21 Ghalib is using the word "Muslim" more as a poetic metaphor for fidelity (good intent) rather than as someone belonging to Islamic religion.

O my helplessness,
longing of my heart!
While I was lamenting,
I remembered the liver.

I would have spent my life
as it is.
Why did I remember
the path
that you traversed?

I will have a fight
with the heaven's gatekeeper
once he knows
that I am trying to reach
your home in there.

Alas!
there is no courage
left to lament!
Having given up on my heart,
I should think of my liver.

Once again
I think of your alley.
I remembered the heart
that I lost there.

This desolation
is like
no other desolation.
When I was in the wilderness
it reminded me
of my home.

I did something
to Majnun
in my boyhood, Asad.
As I picked up a stone,
I remembered
my own head.

NOTHING WRONG BEING A PROFESSIONAL LOVER

If there was delay
in your coming,
there must be a reason.
Wonder,
who held you back?

I can't unjustly
blame you
for my devastation.
There is no doubt
that my fate too
had a hand in it.

May I remind you
if you fail to think of me?
Remember the catch
tied to the stirrup
of your saddle?

The memory
of your tresses
saddened your maniac lover

in the prison,
though the heaviness
of the chains
was also a factor.

Why make a fuss
about the lightening that struck
in front of my eyes?
You should have talked to me
as I was dying to say something.

When I described
her resemblance to Joseph,
it was met with silence.
Imagine the punishment
if the likeness
was really off beat!

When I saw you
with the other guy,
it made me frigid and chilly.
His inability
to commune with you
though was a source
of some satisfaction.

Without blaming Farhad,
there is nothing wrong
being a professional lover.
He was a lunatic like us,
though little too inexperienced.

I was standing there,
ready to die,

but she didn't approach me.
Am I right in guessing
that there was no arrow
left in her quiver?

We are unfairly caught
based on the testimony
of angels watching us.
Should we not expect God
to look at the testimony
of a fellow human as well?

You're not the sole virtuoso
of the craft of ghazal writing, Ghalib!
People say that in the times gone by,
there was someone named Mir[22]
as well.

A LIVING MONUMENT

I'm the living monument
to those lovers who died
thirsty lipped
in the pursuit of the passion
of their life!

Always despairing,
always skeptical

[22] Mir Taqi Mir (1723-1810). Mir was a leading Urdu poet of the 18th century who pioneered the art of ghazal writing in Urdu.

I am the heart of those
who have been stung
by faithlessness.

A TEAR IN THE LOVER'S EYE

You have not been
anyone's friend,
What you did to others,
you have done to me.

Just as the fabled moon
seen in Nakhshab[23]
was no match
to the real moon,
nature couldn't create a sun
to match your moonlike beauty.

Since the beginning of time,
ability is seen
to accompany courage.
A drop can become a pearl,
but that is nothing
like becoming a tear
in the lover's eye.

Until I realized the splendor
of my beloved's presence,
I did not believe

---

23 An artificial moon seen in the town of Nakhshab.

how she could be the source
of that tumult
on the Day of Resurrection.

As a simple hearted person,
I react happily to the display
of anger by the beloved.
I do not need
a repeat of the lesson
on how to subdue my desire.

The river of my sins
dried up
for shortage of water.
Sadly, not even the edge
of my garb
had become wet.

My heart has been on fire
for a long time, Asad,
though the fireplace inside
has not yet turned itself
into a room for salamander.[24]

RED COLORED HENNA

Last night
she bared herself
and the candle wick
emitted so much heat

24 A legendary lizard-like creature that lives in fire and dies when taken out of fire.

that the chandelier
turned itself into a thorn
between the candle
and the beloved.

The red color in henna
comes from the blood
of your martyred lover.
How much, O God,
am I a victim
of my own desire for intimacy!

The outcome of my love
has not seen anything
but a defeat of desire.
When two hearts are united,
they give the appearance
of two sad lips.

What can you make me say
of the leisurely ailment
of my heart?
Whatever I eat
turns itself into blood
bypassing stages
of the digestive process.

AN IMAGE IN THE MIRROR

When she looked herself
in the mirror,
her defenses fell apart.

She gave her heart away
though she had been
its proud custodian,

Please do not try
to slay the messenger
with the crushing
move of your hand.
The poor fellow is not at fault.
I wrote that letter to you.

THE WISDOM OF SIX DIRECTIONS

My heart is no longer
able to express my love
with joy and affection.
Though it has been my pride,
it no longer functions
like a regular heart.

I leave this world
with a bundle
of unfulfilled longings.
I have been removed
like a burned out candle
from the company
of the living.

I have to think
of some other ways
of killing myself.
With arms and hands

so delicate,
it is an insult
for her to kill me.

I find wisdom
in all six directions,
the work of the Great Magician!
Complete and incomplete,
flawed or flawless
are one and the same.

My passion
to look at her face
has loosened the ribbons
of her veil.
There is no barrier now
with the exception
of my own eyes.

Though I spent
most of my time
trying to make a living,
there never was a time
when you were away
from my thoughts.

The very thought of fidelity
has been uprooted
from my heart.
What remains
are some suffocated
and suppressed desires.

Hardships caused by love
no longer frighten me, Asad.
The heart of which
I was so proud
is not the heart
that I know anymore.

A TAVERN OF UNIVERSAL MYSTERY

My envious heart tells me.
Alas!
She is friends with a stranger.
But intellect tells me,
how could
that unloving person
be a friend of anyone?

Each particle in this cup
is guided by a tavern
of universal mystery
just as Laila's eyes swayed
Majnun's wanderings
in the desert.

Passion gives pride and courage
to the most humble beings.
Just as sand gives
wholeness to the desert
and water makes the ocean.

I'm a bad news
because I'm the owner

of a wild heart --
an enemy of comfort
and a lover of loitering.

Jealousy is an emotion
that is best kept to ourselves.
My head is in my knees
while you are looking
in the mirror!

Asad, Farhad was engraving
an image of Shirin.
But hitting his head on the stone
didn't bring him
closer to the beloved.

A HOUSE HIGHER THAN THE HEAVEN

Talking to my confidant
about her angelic beauty
became a threat.
Someone I thought was my friend
suddenly turned into my rival.

I found her drunk
in the company
of my rival.
Was she trying to show me
how much she could drink?

I wanted to build
my house at a great height,

visible from far away.
But my ambition
placed it
higher than the heavens.

I take the insults,
from the person
who guards her place,
in good humor.
She probably doesn't know
that he is an old buddy!

How long can I go on writing
about the anguish of my heart?
My fingers are wounded
and my pen is dripping
with blood.

Slowly, I would have rubbed it off
with my prostrations.
That stone
at your threshold --
why did you replace it?

So that he doesn't speak
ill of me,
I have struck friendship
with my rival.
Making him a confidant
I thought was the best way.

I didn't have the wisdom
of a philosopher
nor was I proficient

in any other skill.
The Heaven
turned against me, Ghalib,
for no reason.

ANTIMONY FOR THE EYES

My value
is nothing more than antimony
for the eyes
which is a free give away.
If people see better
they will realize
I've done something good
for them.

O my oppressive love,
please allow me
to show my grief.
Your face is actually showing
how you're reacting
to my hidden pain.

A MOTH KNOWS HOW TO DIE

People are lost
in their own egoistic mind
and fail to know
that a blade of grass

flutters only
on the shoulders
of breeze.

Drinking in the tavern
doesn't bring
the pleasure
that is everlasting.
Happiness is more like the prey
that is ready to escape.

It is possible that God
might accept explanation
for my sins.
A simple admission
without shame or an apology.

I walk to the altar of sacrifice
in complete ecstasy.
The thought of wounds
is vanquished
by the vision of flowers.

Asad, I breathe
with the hope
of getting her last glance.
A moth knows
how to die
without commotion
in the candle's fiery glow.

A TIDE OF BLOOD

You promised
to give up cruelty
but how?
You say, "I'm too mortified
to show my face."

The seven heavens
are in constant motion,
day and night.
Something will happen
but that's no reason to worry.

Enmity could be taken
for affection.
A matter of interpretation.
But if there is nothing there,
what could I say?

Why did I stalk, O God,
my own letter carrier?
Was I trying to deliver
my letter to her personally?

Even if there is a tide of blood
going over my head,
that is not a good reason
to leave my beloved's door?

I spent my life waiting
as death approached me.
Lo and behold, I died.
Now, what?

There are those
who want to know
all about Ghalib.
Say something.
But what could I possibly say
about myself?

FINENESS WITHOUT CRUDENESS

There is no manifestation
of fineness
without crudeness.
Garden is like a mirror coating
displaying images
of spring breeze.

River bank keeps its pride
until the rising tide breaks it.
When Saqi is around,
my effort to stay sober
is such a waste.

THE COLORS OF REALITY

A drop of water
falling into the river
finally becomes the river.
When the pain exceeds its limits,
it becomes its own remedy.

Our relationship,
due to bad luck,
had the appearance
of a coded lock.
Separation happened
when things were
really looking up.

The poor heart
got crushed
in our struggle
to resolve our differences.
It got rubbed off
in its effort
to resolve the mystery
of our relationship.

Now, she has stopped
being cruel to me,
O God!
Has our enmity reached a point
where even cruelty
has to be denied?

My crying in grief
turned my breath cold.
Believe me
there were tears
but they turned
into vapors.

For me to forget
the thought
of your henna colored fingers
is like separating
nails from the flesh.

When the sky is clear
after the spring clouds
have rained,
it's just like my extinction
after crying
in the sorrow of separation.

If the fragrance of flowers
is not lusting
to reach your alley,
then why is it sprinting
with the breezy dust in the path
leading to your place?

So that it reveals the secret
of how things
need polishing and shining,
the mirror in the rainy season
becomes green
and needs cleaning.

The splendor of flowers, Ghalib,
makes us appreciate beauty.
The eye should be able to see reality
in the colors
in which it reveals itself.

WHEN WINE GETS WINGS

This is the time
once again
when wine gets wings
and starts to fly.
While I'm cautiously waiting,
I want the decanter
to float toward me.

I don't know why
those who live
in the garden are drunk.
The breeze that passes
under the grapevines
might have the taste
of wine.

If you had too much to drink,
consider yourself fortunate.
Even if it gets over your head,
you will fly like huma.[25]

Anything playful can happen
in the rainy season.
The cool breeze brings good cheer
and the air is like
a joyous wave of wine.

There are four tides rising
and coming toward me

---

25 Huma is a legendary bird that brings good luck to the one who is able to walk under its shadow.

from four directions.
Tides of flowers,
twilight, breeze, and wine.

As the soul of the plants
makes them eager to bloom,
wine comforts our soul
to do the same
and bloom as humans.

It is running like blood
in the veins of the grapevine.
Because of its color
it has covered the whole place
with its tresses.

The abundance of flowers
has lighted the pathway
of my imagination.
But my thoughts are filled
with the expectation
of wine tasting.

Behind the mask
of intoxication,
the wine is scanning my mind.
Indirectly,
it is helping me to grow
my intellect and be fruitful.

From the greenery of the grass
to the wave of wine,
the intensity is stirring
a storm all around.

The joy of life owes its existence
to the season of flowers.
The wave of wine is telling
a drop of water
how to unite with the ocean.

Asad, looking at the beauty
of flowers, I lose my senses.
Once again,
it's time to open wine's tresses
and let them flow freely.

Part Three

As I lay dying
my eyes closed,
and I tried to keep them open.
Alas!
What a terrible time
my friends chose
to bring her
to my bedside!

W*rong Timing* [p. 124] is a single couplet ghazal. If we treat it as a poem of 8 lines in its free verse translation, we can easily find three things: a context, a storyline, and a dramatic ending. The context is arrival of death. The physical condition is such that the poet can't keep his eyes open. The storyline is a long love affair in which the poet invited his beloved to visit his abode but without any success. But thanks to the merciful intervention by his friends the beloved is now visiting her lover who is on his deathbed. The dramatic ending is the act of dying in which the lover is neither able to see nor speak to his last-minute visitor. There is also a mystical dilemma in these few words: We passionately desire something; it is like a mirage that we are running after. Then one day our wish is fulfilled but somehow it is too late and meaningless. These are the games that fate plays with us and we have to go through it notwithstanding the pain and suffering it might cause.

This couplet from *No String, No Rosary* [p. 134] reveals Ghalib's thinking about socially defined religious differences.

Tie the holy string up
that hangs around the neck.
Break the circular rosary
of one hundred beads.
A traveler can walk smoothly
when the path is even.

Hindus wear a string around their neck as a symbol of the Hindu way of life. Muslims, on the other hand, use a rosary of 99 beads, called Tasbeeh or Masbaha, to keep track of counting of the Names of Allah. The hand movement on the rosary however is not as smooth as the ordinary string since fingers have to jump from one bead to another. The poet poses a rhetorical question: What would happen if we remove the beads? We will be left with a simple and plain string, just like the one which Hindus use. Ghalib, consistent with his belief in the unity of all human beings, uses religious artifacts that at some level put people in different boxes, but if we look deeper we find that what unites people of different faiths is more significant than what divides them. The word "traveler" or *rahro* (in the original) in the second part of couplet could be taken to mean one's higher self that transcends religious differences. One moves faster towards one's destination when the guiding spirit takes charge and conventional ritualism takes a back seat.

There are several compositions in this part that carry both unity of form as well as similarity of content and thus they qualify to be called poems in the traditional sense. These include *Today* [p. 127], *Be Patient* [p. 128], *When I'm Gone* [p. 129], *Walls And Doors* [p. 131], and *No Need to Say This* [p. 133].

Today starts with a positive note saying that the beloved is coming to visit the garden and that there are special arrangements to be made to welcome her. What kind of arrangements? The gate to the garden will have a lock to restrict access to it by the ordinary folks. Where does this lock come from? Ghalib stretches the reader's imagination by suggesting that the lock was nothing other than the ring around turtledove's neck.

Why turtledove? Because she is in love with the moon and her gaze is always fixed at the sky. The rest of the poem is quite pessimistic with the last line suggesting that such is the flood of lover's tears today that it was demolishing the doors and walls of his house.

Be Patient is significant because patience is not a lover's better-known qualities. He has a heart that is always impatient. The poet is making a case for patience and includes routine things like patiently waiting for the wine to be served, keeping poise when the appreciation for an action fails to materialize. Ghalib dips into two cognitive metaphors (narcissus and salamander), which are part of mythologies that evoke a sense of awe. Narcissus as a flower is poetically depicted as the one without an eye or a heart, though it always looks with a sense of awe at the beloved. Imagine a flower gazing without an eye! The poet uses the metaphor to make fun of the rival who is a person of no deep insight. Standing next to the beloved, he is unable to appreciate her beauty unlike the flower. Salamander is a mythical creature that lives in fire. Imagine eating kabobs made of salamander's heart! Lover is hungry but it is a hunger for the vision of the beloved, not of a body part of a creature that doesn't even exist.

When I'm Gone imagines a grim future when the poet has passed away ("The flame of love will die after me"). The reason for this pessimistic assessment is not that one person (or one lover) has died. People die and they are easily forgotten. What then is unusual about this death? The poem provides an answer: When the poet died, the best of what we call love also died with him. The arts of flattery and seduction died with him. But there is so much left after his demise. That is why the poet wonders at the end: Whose house this unfulfilled yearning of love will destroy after his death!

Walls And Doors is an excellent poem in which the poet reifies walls and doors of his home. They are not walls and doors any more. They are the living entities and they share the passion of the owner. They are also in love with the beloved. When they heard that the beloved was in the neighborhood, they stepped forward to welcome her. They were falling over one another to have a glimpse of her and to welcome her. The poem ends on a rather sad note: Don't tell anyone that Ghalib has died. This secret is safe with the walls and doors.

No Need To Say This is a string of several routine and non-routine observations. The poet relocated himself at the beloved's doorsteps and she didn't even notice the change. The underlying theme: she just doesn't pay any attention to what the lover is doing.

FINGERS

Alas!
Fingers are now used
to give food to the teeth to chew.
Fingers that were lucky once
to play with strings of pearls.

You decided not to give me
your ring as a souvenir.
You showed me the bare finger
when you moved away from me.

Asad, the fire inside
makes me write words full of warmth.
No one should point a finger
at my words.

LONG LIVE!

Even if someone lived
until the Day of Resurrection,
death would still come
because we die one day.[26]

---

26 The poet is addressing Khizr or Khidr, a revered figure in Islam, who was given the gift of eternal life.

In the agony of my suffering,
I'm passionately drinking blood
and my liver writes in all humility,
"O Thank You God!"

Unlike my pathetic rival
I'm ready to be a martyr
in pursuit of love.
Bravo. Kudos. Long live!

I can't make sense of things
as they appear to be.
Yet I wish this deceptive
display of reality
to live for a long time.

WRONG TIMING

As I lay dying
my eyes closed,
and I tried to keep them open.
Alas!
What a terrible time
my friends chose
to bring her
to my bedside!

FRIEND

As hair started showing up
on my friend's face,
it looked smoked out.
It was nothing more than a streak
on the cheek, but
why did the untrue friends flee?

O reckless heart,
control yourself.
Who can withstand the radiance
of my friend's beauty?

See how this spectacle
of my friend's beauty
has destroyed peoples' homes.
As a footprint, I have no choice;
I go where the friend goes.

Jealousy
of what my rival was getting
was my undoing.
I was killed
by my enemy's actions
though I was already sick
in my friend's love.

I'm pleased
that the heart of my uncaring lover
is at peace at last.
My eyes are bloodshot though,
filled with the wine
of my friend's eyes.

When the misery of separation
from my friend
reaches a tipping point,
a stranger comes
and consoles me.
He could be a friend
who is also suffering
the pangs of separation.

I don't know how close is my rival
to you, my friend
but he brings me your message.
I'm shattered if this is true.
I'm also shattered
if he just made it up.

When I talk with you
about my brain's malfunction,
you my friend
start talking about your hair
and the air is perfumed.

If my rival finds me crying
and in a desperate state of mind,
he smilingly narrates
a witty conversation
he has had with you, my friend.

Should I complain
about the kindness
of my enemy?
Or should I express gratitude
about how, my friend, you
are tormenting me?

In the last line
of each couplet of this ghazal
which he wrote,
Ghalib repeats one word
and the word is "friend."[27]

TODAY

Today
The colors and shades of the garden
are arranged differently.

Today
Even the ring on the turtledove's neck
is the latch on the gate.

Today
With each high-pitched cry of pain,
a piece of my heart comes off as well.
It's like throwing away the noose
to catch a prey.

Today
The doors and walls of my home
are flooded with my tears.
Say goodbye to everything
that was arranged
to keep the house standing.

---

27 It appears that this ghazal was written for a male lover.

A REMEDY FOR LOVE SICKNESS

Lo,
there is hope for those
suffering from love sickness.
But if they don't get well,
can they really blame
the Messiah?

BE PATIENT

Be patient
Don't breathe
outside the boundaries
of what you really want.
If there is no wine,
just wait for your turn.

Be patient
Don't ask
why there is no appreciative eye
for your efforts.
Remove the lines
from your mirror
like you remove thorns.

Be patient
You want an excuse
to rest a while,
O my lazy heart!

Who has given you the signal
to overindulge
while you rest on my bed?

Be patient
The flowering narcissus
is looking at her with envy.
My rival is without a heart or an eye
like a narcissus.
I can drink to that.

Be patient
Return the debt that you owe her
with a romantic glance.
Take the dagger out
from the veil of your body
and return it gratefully to its owner.

Be patient
In the inner recesses of my body
lies the wine of hidden fire.
I long for kabobs
made of the heart of salamander.

• •

WHEN I AM GONE

When I am gone
Beauty will cease its flirtatious moves.
Those who oppressed me
will finally be at peace.

When I am gone
The ranks of truly mad lovers
will thin out and the elegance
of unbridled longing will lose
its crown jewel.

When I am gone
The flame of love will die after me.
Smoke rises while the candle dies,
leaving nothing behind,
just a garb of pure blackness.

When I am gone
My heart will bleed at her dismay
while I rest in my grave.
Her nails will frantically search
for henna that my blood once supplied.

When I am gone
No one, who is qualified,
will be left behind to face her cruelty.
Her eyes will search for someone
to get mad at.

When I am gone
My wildness will bid farewell
to the lovers and lunatics.
The art of slitting the garb
will be lost after me..

When I am gone
Saqi will call out men
and dare them to drink
the wine of love.

Her lips will repeat the call
but in vain.

When I am gone
Sorrow will kill me
and there will be no one
in the world to ask the question:
who will mourn the death of love
and faithfulness the way I did?

When I am gone
I will cry at the helplessness
of love, Ghalib.
Whose house will this flood ruin
after my death?

WALLS AND DOORS

Walls and doors
I'll bring them down if they blocked my view.
My eyes long to see lovers, feathers, and wings.

Walls and doors
Look at what my tears did to my home.
My walls and doors are now reduced to just
walls and doors.

Walls and doors
It's not the shadow of my walls and doors
that you will see outside.
It's them standing there as they heard
the good news of your plan to visit me.

Walls and doors
Imagine, the abundance of the wine of your spectacle
that walls and doors in your alley
are swaying like a drunk.

Walls and doors
If you are in a mood to shop, stop waiting.
You have a market full of eyes at your doorsteps.

Walls and doors
How did they know that I planned to cry?
Fearing the flooding, they begged me not to do so.

Walls and doors
Really a silly lot!
Since she was visiting my neighborhood,
they showed love, by extending their shadows,
with the neighbor's walls and doors.

Walls and doors
Thanks to the loneliness caused by your absence,
my home is wounding my eyes.
I'm always in tears while looking
at the walls and doors.

Walls and doors
Ask not my ecstatic joy when the flood arrives.
Walls and doors dance too in triumph, head to head.

Walls and doors
Don't tell anyone that Ghalib is no longer in this world.
The secret of loving and dying is however safe
with walls and doors.

NO NEED TO SAY THIS

No need to say this
I made my home at your doorsteps.
If you still do not notice the change,
should I point this out to you?

No need to say this
You asked me how did I lose
my poetic sensibility.
"How could I know what was going on
with your heart, without your telling me?"

No need to say this
What a difficult position I find myself in.
I have to deal with the one
whose name no one utters
without calling her an oppressor.

No need to say this
There is nothing in my heart to say,
lest I would say it
without the fear of losing my head.

No need to say this
I will not stop adoring that idol
though I'm aware of the risks.
Let them call me an infidel.
So be it!

No need to say this
When we talk about her flirting ways
and amorous glances,

we can't proceed
without a talk about knives and daggers.

Needless to say this
Any talk about God should not involve
wine and drinking, but we need the worldly stuff
to make our heads spin before we drink deeply
the heavenly brew.

Needless to say this
I'm hard of hearing and thus
deserving of double kindness.
I understand nothing unless it is repeated.

Needless to say this
Ghalib, please stop whining
in the presence of His Majesty.
Do you really have to explain
what sorry state you are in?
Isn't it plain for him to see?

NO STRING, NO ROSARY

I looked at your face
and I wasn't set ablaze.
I marvel at my strength
to see you standing there
and not turn myself
into a ball of fire.

Worldly people call me
a fire-worshipper.

They may have seen my letters
that emit fire
and reached a conclusion.

Love loses its sanctity
when the pain of playing around
becomes commonplace.
I stop and pull myself away from you
because you inflict pain
without any reason.

She is coming to kill me
but I'm dying in any case.
I'm jealous of the sword
that she holds in her hand.
What a lucky sword!

On the neck of the decanter
there is blood of ordinary people.
Did she kill them
when she had too much to drink?
The wine is trembling,
moving to and fro,
watching her walk
under the influence.

It's really sad
that she has put an end
to her cruelty.
Was I too greedy
in loving my affliction?

We sell ourselves
along with our couplets.

But it also depends
on the temperament
of the buyer.

Tie the holy string up
that hangs around the neck.
Break the circular rosary
of one hundred beads.
A traveler can walk smoothly
when the path is even.

I was distressed to see
the blisters on my feet,
but when I saw thorns
on my way
I was relieved --
my suffering
was coming to an end.

Looking into the rusty mirror
with green spots on it
was risky.
She came from behind
and saw reflection of parrots.

The lightening
should have struck me,
and not the Mount Sinai.
But we get to drink
what is proportional
to our capacity.

When I looked at your wall,
I remembered

a nutcase named Ghalib.
Didn't he strike his head against it
in the fury and agony
of his mad love for you?

RESURRECTION

My heart quivers
at the task
that hot and bright sun
is being asked to perform.
I'm just a drop of dew
that is hanging onto a thorn
in the wilderness.

Joseph spread the light around
with his virtuous presence,
as he always did.
His father Jacob's wandering eyes
felt the whiteness
farway in his prison cell.

I have mastered the art of ecstasy
from the time long past.
To be precise,
when Majnun was scribbling alphabet
on the walls of his school.

I would have been free
from the anxiety
to find a treatment

for my ailment
if the pieces of my broken heart
were at peace with the saltshaker.

In the entire field of courtship
there is nothing written
that doesn't carry the stamp
of my beloved's musings
on the subject.

Looking at the colorful sky
I remembered,
when I waited for you
in the garden
at the time of our separation,
and how sparks of fire
used to rain on the flowers.

What else would have survived
except the uncontrollable desire
for the one you loved?
Resurrection is nothing
but the fast wind blowing
the ashes of lovers.

Don't pick up a pointless fight
with the preacher Ghalib.
Forget that he had spoken
some harsh words to you.
If you're looking
for dressing something down,
think of the shirt you're wearing.

HEARTS ON SALE

She does send me
conflicting signals.
There are hidden meanings
in her gestures.
Even her words of love
suggest concealed motives.

O God!
Will she ever understand
what I'm trying to tell her.
She needs another heart
and I need another way
to communicate my feelings.

There is no connection
between her way of seeing
and her eyebrows.
There is an arrow
that you see but not know
where the bow is.

When you are in town
and your lovers are desperate,
there is little for me to worry about.
I can go to the market
and buy one of the hearts on sale.

Although I've been good
in breaking idols
that I once worshipped,

my path is long and arduous
and there are other heavy stones
on the way.

My liver is boiling over
with blood
and I would have shed
blood-soaked tears
with great abandon
if I had more than
two eyes.

I'm dying to listen to her voice
though my head
is about to be separated
from my body.
She is telling the executioner,
"Yes, more."

When I show them
a new wound each day,
people often confuse them
with the sun.
Such is the luminosity
of my abrasions!

If I had not given
my heart to you
I would have found
some peace of mind.
And if I had not died
I would have done
less of moaning and wailing.

When the water flow
is obstructed,
the level of water goes up
and it finds
forceful openings.
When my emotions are blocked,
they too find
forceful openings.

The world is full of poets
of great literary merit.
Each one better than the other.
But Ghalib's style of recitation,
they say, is in a class by itself.

CHANGE

A mirror gets rusted
with the passage of time.
Water changes its composition
and allows algae to grow
when it is stagnant.

Comforts of life didn't cure
my lunatic tendencies.
Even the bowl
studded with diamonds
for drinking wine
reminded me of leapord's spots
and the wilderness.

NAKED MADNESS

How do you express
your madness if you're
not naked?
The slit in my shirt
made the task easier
and my neck cleared its debt.

The state of my inner commotion
is like burning of a paper
that turns and curls
while it goes up in smoke.
The thousand mirrors of my heart
fly on the wings of despair
just like the fumes
of the burning words.

Time has stolen
the luxuries that we enjoyed
in the days gone by.
The robber thinks differently.
What was once stolen
is not something
that is owed back
to the owner.

Talk about paranoia.
She thinks
that the sunrays falling on her face
from the slits of her window
are coming from
my eyes watching her.

Surrender yourself to extinction
if you want to know your reality.
The waste gets luckier
when it is thrown
into the furnace of love.

What kind of wounded person
is Asad really?
He is telling the killer,
"Please go on practicing
the art of seduction.
The burden of this killing
is on my neck and shoulders."

DREAMING OF A MALE LOVER

I suffer the pain and anguish
for a reason.
Beautiful men are in love with you.
Niceties aside,
if I'm lucky
then I too will get a lover
like them, finally.

ON DEATH AND DYING

I wanted you to wait for me
before you died.[28]
Since you made your choice,
you will have to live alone
for some days more.

By rubbing my forehead
no damage will be done to the stone.
My head will have to take the hit.
Then I repeat the same act again.
I will rub my forehead at your door
for some days more.

You came yesterday
and you want to leave today.
Agreed that time doesn't stand still.
For some days more – stay.

You tell me while you leave.
We shall meet again
on the Doomsday.
Is there another Doomsday
besides this one?

O God, Arif was still very young.
What harm could have been done
if he had lived
for some days more.

28 This ghazal was written in Arif's memory. He was Ghalib's wife's nephew and his adopted son who died young.

You were the full moon light
of my home.
But then you left suddenly.
The aura of light
would have stayed in the house
if you had stayed
for some days more.

You were not steadfast
in what you had to say.
The angel of death
would have allowed you to live
for some days more.

You had mixed feelings about me
and fights with Nayyar,
you should have lived
to see the children play
for some days more.

There were good days and bad,
but why die so young?
You should have lived
for some days more.

You showed your innocence
when you asked Ghalib:
why do you continue to live?
My fate will fulfill my wish to die
but after living for some days more.

NOTHING MORE TO GIVE

Don't think
death has freed me
like the sun and the morning.
My shroud
still carries the scars of love.

I'm like a poor man
who takes pride
in having lost his wealth.
I'm like a flower-seller
who is trying to show
his chronic scars.

In the tavern of my liver
there is not even a drop of dust
left to give.
Why is she asking
for more to drink
with signs of hangover?

THE TAVERN OF INSANITY

Prayer did not resolve
my predicament.
May God let Khizr
live a long life!

Wandering in the wilderness
doesn't resolve
the mystery of life.

Our thoughts have to walk slowly
through many peaks and valleys.

Her beauty is on display,
but my mind is somewhere else.
I've been polishing the crystal ball
waiting for her to arrive.

Each particle of lover's ashes
is worshipping the sun.
Though nothing more than
a pile of dust,
its lust for union remains strong.

Ghalib, please do not ask me
about the expanse
of the tavern of insanity.
It is bigger than heaven
which is nothing more than
a dustbin of humans.

RAINDROPS LIKE PEARLS

His benevolence
is all around us.
Clouds filled with water
remind us of blistered feet
and raindrops fall
like pearls from the sky.

The marks
on the burned out pages

in the book of wilderness
make my footsteps run faster
in that direction.

THE TIP OF YOUR ARROW

How can I save my soul
from the one I love and adore
when the true meaning of what I believe
is to give my life to her?

When you looked at me,
your arrow hit my heart.
I tried to take it out,
but I want to leave it there.
The tip of your arrow
is dear to me.

Ghalib, you need to be patient
and accept what is happening.
The incident is severe.
But your life is dear to you.
Isn't it?

AN OBITUARY

I am neither a delightful melody
nor a musical arrangement.
I am the voice of my own defeat.

While you were busy
embellishing your tresses,
I was filled with fear
thinking of what the future
might have in store for us.

It's my simplicity to boast
that I can fully control myself.
But the secret buried in my chest
must come out sooner or later.

I'm a prisoner of a bird-catcher,
though I haven't lost my strength
to simply fly away.

I wish I see the day
when my tormentor reveals
her true beauty
instead of my hoping
endlessly for that to happen.

In my heart I do not have
that drop of blood
that turns my eyelashes
into a sport of flowers.

Your sultry and seductive look
is totally intoxicating
and the way you inflict pain
is unmatched head to toe.

You displayed
your charm and beauty.
Congratulations!

My forehead is lowered
in humility.

You inquired my well-being.
It was kind but no big deal.
I'm the poor wanderer
and you're my caretaker.

Asad Ulla Khan.
Sorry to tell you
that he has died.
Alas!
What a drunkard
and a womanizer!

A LONGING FOR CAPTIVITY

Congratulations!
My longing for captivity
can now see
that the net is empty
for the one who likes to keep the bird
in a cage.

My liver's craving
for receiving more pain
was not fulfilled,
though I gave out
a river of blood
at the root of
every thorny bush.

My eyes closed
as soon as they opened.
Alas! Alas!
What a time did you select
to visit your love sick!

I would not have died
at a slow pace
if the one who consoled me
had a sharp dagger
instead of a sharp tongue.

You can go and relax
in the mouth of a lion,
but my heart,
just listen to me,
and do not stand next to the beauty
that devastates you.

Seeing you
the flowers in the garden
shoot up.
Without any push,
they vie with one another
to reach the edge
of your headdress.

Ghalib, the wild one,
died by smashing his head.
Alas! Alas!
Remember, his coming to your wall
and sitting there.

BEAUTY AND THE MIRROR

The house of mirrors
would have burned down
if the greenish moisture
from her face
had not moved to the mirror
to save it.

Her dazzling appearance
resolved the lover's dilemma.
If the wick,
which is like a thorn in the candle,
didn't burn,
there would be no residue
at the candle's feet.

SUNSET

The rays of the evening sun
show the path
it would take to go down.
A crescent appears in the sky
to embrace the sun
and to say farewell.

Part Four

It takes a long time
for my groans and moans
to show some result.
I can't live long enough
to conquer your tresses.

A *Remedy For The Pain Of Life* [p. 158] is a very popular ghazal. Several great singers have sung it. The ghazal seamlessly weaves the challenges of being in love and the vicissitudes of life that cause endless suffering. Sighs or laments take a lifetime to come to fruition. Life is just too short for a lover to get close to the beloved's "tresses." Why tresses? Because they are like chains that bind the lover. Also when the lover is close to the tresses, it is a sign that he has reached a point that could open up chances of sensual intimacy. But since this possibility could be viewed as love's final realization, the poet makes a point that it can't happen in this life. With this twist, this couplet gives us a completely new meaning. The love we talk about here has to be placed at a much higher plane – it is a yearning for a form of love that is clearly beyond the human domain. A similar thought is expressed in the fourth couplet: "granted that you will never be indifferent to my love but the speed at which you reveal your love and care for me, I will be reduced to a pile of ash." The last three couplets are a meditation on the length of life, which under circumstances of hardship appears too long. No, it is not long at all, the poet says. He compares life to a dewdrop that evaporates when the sun comes out. It is like a wink of an eye, or the dance of a spark. Until the day when death arrives (which finally puts an end to human suffering) life flickers like the flame of a candle, showing various colors, until the time it is morning again (which could mean death or redemption).

It Is All Gone [p. 164] is a beautiful poem of remembrance – one of Ghalib's favorite themes.

Where are those pangs of separation
and those moments of union?
Where are those days and evenings
and where are those months and years?

The journey of love has come to an end. The poet explains in the last couplet how the old age and loss of balance in the body's elements have made "loving" difficult. Yet it is not a clean slate. There is no pain of separation and no joy of the union. Yet embers of the fire that once burned still survive. Some things have become a part of the memory but the poet is conflicted about how much "love" remains.

Ghalib Has Died [p. 166] has one couplet that says something important about Ghalib's concept of God.

The One whom we call upon
is beyond the limits of human wisdom.
Kaaba is merely a pointer
to the direction of our prayers.

Human beings try to find God within the material context because it is so convenient. Seeing God in solid objects like stones or idols also uplifts human spirit. But these things, as Ghalib says, have little significance other than as directional pointers or as a compass. Kaaba tells us which way to pray. But if we are in search of God, we have to look for Him in all places and in all directions. It is also possible that we might find Him deep inside our own being. "Inside" is also one of the directions that we need to pursue.

THE CANDLE

The candle sees the beloved
and out of sheer envy
it burns itself.
The radiance of her cheeks
offers the candle
the passion to live
while constantly burning itself.

In the words of linguists,
death is silence.
This was demonstrated
in her assembly
in the dying words
of the candle.

The candle's story
comes to an end
at the very hint of a flame.
The story is that of self-annihilation,
as told by the candle.

She is grieving the fate
of the moth, O Flame!
The candle's sorrow is seen
from its flickering.

Your very thought
makes my soul swirl in ecstasy.

Just like the wind whirling around
the candle's flame.

Don't ask me
about the joyful spring
of love's scars.
There is freshness in the remnants
after the candle burns out.

She burns with jealousy
after seeing me standing
by my beloved's bedside.
Why shouldn't my heart carry the scar
of the candle's erratic behavior?

ALAS!

Cautious
that my rival is keeping a tab,
I do not want to lose my senses.
O my inner controller,
take note
how badly you constrain me?
Alas!

My heart broods
why didn't I burn myself
in one try.
O the incompetence
of my fire emitting breath!
Alas!

SALT

The heartless kids are spraying salt
at my worn out wounds.
I would have enjoyed it more
if the stones thrown at me
had salt in them.

The dust of her alley brings comfort
to my heart's malaise.
Otherwise, where else in this world
you would find that much salt.

May I go on getting it freely!
May you live long!
The pain of nightingale's cry
and salt in the blooming
of flowers.

When she came to the beach
riding her sand-kicking horse,
the waves felt the challenge,
and the sand turned into salt.

Bravo!
She really thinks highly
of the wounds of my liver
and she calls to her mind
my condition
whenever she sees salt.

To leave behind
the wounded body of a lover
is really sad.

The heart is in love with the wounds
but the body wants salt.

I don't need any stranger's help
to increase my pain.
My wounds liked the smile on her face
before she struck me
and they are completely filled with salt.

Ghalib, do you remember those days
when in the ecstasy of desire,
you lifted the salt
falling off your wounds
with your eyelashes?

A REMEDY FOR THE PAIN OF LIFE

It takes a long time
for my groans and moans
to show some result.
I can't live long enough
to conquer your tresses.

The open mouths
of one-hundred crocodiles
are ready to trap
every incoming wave.
We have to wait
and see what happens to a drop
before it becomes a pearl.

Love demands patience,
but desire wants satisfaction.
Should I listen to my heart
wanting everything
or go with my liver
which is telling me to wait
and be patient?

I'm not saying
you won't care for me
if malady strikes me.
But at the speed you get the news
I will be a pile of ashes
by the time you know about it.

The dew learned its lesson
of extinction from the brightness
of the sun's rays.
I too wait for someone's kindness,
to turn her gaze toward me.

Life ends in the wink of an eye,
O my ignorant self!
The life of a gathering is
no longer than the dance
of the spark of the light.

O Asad, what is the remedy
for the pain of life except death?
The candle has to burn
until the sun comes out
and it is morning once again.

THE COUNT OF MY SINS

Do not pray for a small thing
if you are convinced
of the power of the prayer.
And do not pray at all
unless your heart is free
from desire.

Remembering the wounds
that I suffered in the pursuit
of my heart's desires,
ask me not, O God,
the count of my sins.

FLOWERS

Flowers are cheating
on nightingale
giving her false assurance
of their fidelity.
They are really in love with you
and the gullible nightingale
doesn't know it.

Felicitations, O Breeze,
as you are free to move
unrestrained.
Flowers are broken
because the spring is over
and their scent is gone.

Alas!
The sturdy one
so proud of its color died too.
Wailing on the dried lips of flowers
invites blood-soaked sighs
from the onlookers.

Lucky is the lover
who in a state of ecstasy
keeps his head
at the edge of flowers
and virtually becomes their shadow.

Spring invents everything for you.
Talk of my new rival.
The fragrance of flowers!

They are shaming me
in the face of spring breeze.
A decanter without any wine in it
and a heart
that has lost its lust for flowers.

Compared to the awe-inspiring
pageant of your beauty,
the parade of flowers
is nothing more than the blood
in my eyes.

It is the allure
of your breathtaking splendor
that we have until now
flowers running amuck

back to back
to please you.

Ghalib,
I have this burning desire
to embrace her –
whose very thought
is like decorating the flower
sewn on my gown's pocket
with a real flower.

IN A CHAMBER OF MOTH'S HEART

People with a free-mind
do not lose their cheerfulness
even for a fleeting moment.
They light candles
in their darkened homes
from the sparks
of the bolt of lightening.

The card-player plays the game
and imagines assemblies of players
who have played and gone.
I stand in the house of idols
flipping pages of a memory book.

Despite the din and noise
of our day to day living,
there is no real joy
in the act of living.

We are like the light
in a chamber of a moth's heart.

We are giving up
on our higher aspirations
not due to a weakness
or a sense of contentment.
We are disgracefully resting
our head on a pillow,
easily giving up on our manliness.

Asad,
millions of longings
have been sentenced for life.
My blood stained chest
has become their prison cell.

A RATTLING SOUND

With the help
of your cries and moans,
make your heart happy.
The real worth of a chain
is nothing but its rattling sound.

DEATH IN A FOREIGN LAND

I was killed in a foreign land,
far away from home.

How kind!
God saved me from destitution.

The curls of her tresses
are waiting for me in ambush,
O God!
Please defend my honor
and my freedom.

THE DEBT OF SLEEP

I am tempted to borrow
from my treasure of sleep
a night full of dreamless sleep.
But Ghalib I'm afraid
how would I pay this debt.

IT IS ALL GONE

Where are those pangs of separation
and those moments of union?
Where are those days and evenings
and where are those months and years?

Where is the time to pursue
the passion of love?
Where is the yearning
to see the march of the beautiful?

Why cry about the heart when
even the mind is gone.
Where is the passion now
to see her curvaceous figure?
It is all gone.

My imagination
created those beautiful images
with inspiration
coming from just one person.
But when she was gone
so was the imagery.

It's not easy to shed blood tears.
But now there is a problem.
My heart has no strength.
And my liver is no longer resolute.

No more the gambler's den of love.
Even if I wanted to go back,
I don't have the money
in my pocket to play the game.

I get headache thinking about
the state of the world.
Who am I? Why am I here?
This is clearly not my cup of tea.

Ghalib, I am weak and old
with no strength left in me.
My body's elements
are in a state of flux
and the things are
far from in the balance.

GHALIB HAS DIED

When she was in love with me,
my rival called it a betrayal.
Isn't there a tradition of bad mouthing
good people?

Today I'm going to level with her.
I'm gung-ho, but just watch
what I actually end up saying.

Don't tell them anything.
These people belong to another age.
A cup of wine and a melody,
they say, makes the stress go away.

I remembered her when I regained
my consciousness.
My prayer was answered
when you returned to my thoughts.

The One whom we call upon
is beyond the limits of human wisdom.
Kaaba is merely a pointer
to the direction of our prayers.

She was sympathetic
looking at the wounds of my feet.
Thorns in her alley, I said,
are herbs of grace
since they make her think of me.

Why should anyone be afraid
of the spark in my heart?

I like this and want the air
to make the flares get bigger.

Let me see what outcome
her vanity brings about.
Whenever she says something,
we praise God for His magnificence.

My buddies Vahshat and Shefta[29]
will probably write elegies
now that Ghalib has died.
Yes, the songster of sad melodies
has finally passed away.

IN THE PRISON OF SORROW

A flower that is not in the garden
lacks integrity.
A dress that doesn't fall down to the lap
lacks stylishness.

My physical weakness
has sapped my bodily strength.
The color has faded
and there is no blood
at the edges.

Particles from the sun's light
have gathered near the windows
of her house.

[29] Two contemporary poets and close friends.

It is the sun that is really stealing looks
at her beauty.

What can I say about the darkness
of the prison of sorrow.
It's pitch dark.
Even the cotton stuffed in the windows
gives the appearance of dawn.

Life draws its force from love
that brings dismal emptiness.
A gathering is without its candle of light
if no lightening is produced
by the thrashing of a crop.

I'm being laughed at
for seeking a simple remedy
for getting my wounds stitched.
My rival thinks there is no pleasure
in having the needle pierce my flesh.

Since I was killed
by her blossoming beauty,
I find my grave full of flowers
and not even a particle of dust
is to be found.

There are new wounds on my body
that are dripping blood.
Even the blood in my body is not free
from its yearning for pain.

Saqi's vanity took a hit
when I drank an ocean

without any hitch.
The wine's vein
is no longer in the decanter's neck
since it too bowed in shame.

It would be a show of feebleness
when physical weakness
squeezes me from all sides.
My body doesn't have room
for a hunched posture.

Why should I complain
about destitution.
in a foreign land, Ghalib,
when there was not much
while I was at home?
To tell you the truth,
I'm a fistful of garden waste.
I wonder why it's not in the dustbin
already.

PLEASE DO NOT SHAME ME

I'm sorry I was unable to write
an ode to her modesty –
one of her many alluring styles
that I call the cause of my death.

The traps of her tresses
give the appearance
of two wide eyes
watching my heart.

Each strand of these tresses
is an eye decorated with antimony.

My million liver-splitting cries
make me who I am.
You are a non-listener.
What more can I say?

My oppressive love,
please do not shame me
in front of my doubts.
Alas, alas! God forbid
if I ever called you unfaithful.

I CAN'T FIND POISON

Call me back in magnanimity
whenever you need me.
I'm not like the time past or departed
that I would fail to return.

In this state of my feebleness
I'm not concerned
with the jeers of my rivals.
Their talk is unlike my head
which I can lift any time I want.

I can't find poison,
my dear tormentor,
otherwise I swear
in the hope of meeting you
that I would take it gladly.

ONE DAY

One day
Be wild and rowdy with me
in a wine-tasting session.
Otherwise, I will poke fun at you
under the guise of drunkenness.

One day
Don't be deceived by the life's lofty ideals.
Hidden in the heights of these ambitions
are the seeds of downfall.

One day
I ran the bills, thanks to my drunken ways.
How foolishly I thought that this was a way
out of my misery!

One day
O my heart!
Please do accept the songs of sorrow
as a blessing!
This instrument of life will
fall silent.

One day
Getting into a brawl is not the style
of my seductive love.
But it did happen.
It was Ghalib who started it.

LIFE FOR ONE KISS

She is hurting me
not because I was unfaithful to her.
It's simple teasing
and not a test.

How can I thank her
for her sweet favor?
She asked me about my well-being
without uttering a word.

I love my oppressor,
and my oppressor
loves me too.
While being not so kind,
she is not unkind.

You can give me an earful,
if not a kiss.
You do have a tongue,
if not the lips.

Although her cruelty
is a matter of great distress,
I'm left with no strength
to bear it any longer.

My soul is asking,
"Is there more?"[30]
My lips are not seeking kindness
from my tormentor.

---

30 This is a reference to a passage from the Koran. Hell was asked, "Are you filled?" Hell replied, "Is there more?"

Rip your heart apart
if it is not already split in two halves.
Sink a knife
into your heart if your eyelids
are not yet dripping blood.[31]

Shame on you, my heart.
Why aren't you the temple of fire?
Shame on you, my heart.
Why isn't your breath spewing fire?

Nothing was lost
due to my madness,
though my house was ruined.
For one hundred yards of land,
I got the whole wilderness.
Not a bad bargain.

You have a question
about the story of my life.
Isn't it strange that you do not see
what is written on my forehead
when I bow before you?

I do get some praise from him
for my poetry, though Gabriel and I
do not share the same language.

She demands my life
just for one kiss.
She knows that Ghalib
is not even half dead yet.

---

31 This is poet's advice to a young, uninitiated lover.

WHIRLING

No argument can prevent me
from wandering in the desert.
There is whirling in my feet,
not a chain.

My desire for wandering
has taken me to a desert
where the tracks in the sand
are like those seen by an eye
in a painting.

The longing for the delights
of pain is unfulfilled.
The path to love's travails
is like the edge
of a sharp sword.

Long live the sadness
of my dismay!
Keep on enduring!
I'm happy
that my complaint proved
ineffective.

I scratch my head
as the wounds of the head
are close to healing.
The pleasure
that I gained from the stones
is making me speechless.

Her kindness
gives me the strength
to make a move.
To offer any excuse at this time
is nothing but shameful.

Ghalib, it is my firm belief,
and Nasikh agrees with me,
that "you're unaware if you do not
believe in Mir." [32]

THE EYE

I do not believe
vision is centered
in the white outer layer
of the eyeball.
There is light
that comes from the dark spots
caused by sighs gathered
in the heart of the eye.

GROUNDED REALITY

Lover's crying is nothing less
than the rain in the rainy season.
I'm not surprised to see

---

32 Nasikh, a poet who was Ghalib's contemporary and a disciple of Mir Taqi Mir. Mir died in 1810 when Ghalib was 13.

flowers blooming
in hundreds of places
inside the walls of the garden.

It is impossible for us
to free ourselves
from the worldly things
in the same way
as living in the garden
but not loving the flowers.
The cypress tree
though free
is grounded
in the same garden.

IF HOPE IS LOST

Love is not a lost cause
by the nature of its being.
Dying for someone
is not like the fruitless fruit
of the willow tree.

Kingdoms come and go.
But wine in the goblet of love
is not inherited
the way Jamshed got the throne.[33]

---

33 Persian King Jamshed believed to be the inventor of wine. The poet is trying to make the point: Wine, unlike the kingdom, is earned through beloved's grace.

You are the reason for all the dazzle
in human existence.
A speck is not seen
without the sun's light.

The news of my secret love affair
will bring her bad publicity.
Otherwise, there is no secret
in my not dying.

Joys of life come to an end,
but I have no such fear
for despairs of life.
They seem to last forever.

Hope keeps us alive.
There goes the old saying.
Imagine my fate
when even hope is lost.

THE PANHANDLERS

Wherever I see
the impressions of your feet –
I see the beds of flowers blooming
in the mythic city of Iram.[34]

My heart is distressed
at the sight of a mole
close to your mouth.

---

[34] Iram is a lost city mentioned in the Koran.

Looking at it
I'm lost as if I was having
a stroll in a world of dreams.

Your cypress-like height
is the cause of frenzy among your lovers.
It is Doomsday when they realize
that they have been cut short.

A real spectacle!
You are looking into the mirror.
Imagine my longing
when I look at you
at that very moment.

Tracking the complaints
of the scars of my heart
is like following the footprints
of night robbers.

Ghalib,
wearing the garb of panhandlers
I watch the spectacle
of the kind and the generous.

I GAVE UP BOOZE

The roaring flames of hell
are like beloved's disposition.
You can call me a kafir
if I don't find comfort
in love's suffering.

How long have I lived
in this terrible world?
It looks even longer
if I take into account
all the nights of separation.

So that I never get to sleep
ever again in my life
waiting for her,
she promised to come
when she appeared
in one of my dreams.

Let me write her another letter
while I wait for the courier to return.
I know what she would write
in reply to my last letter.

When was the last time
I got my turn to drink so quickly?
It's possible Saqi served wine
blended with something else.

For the one who is faithless,
the magical charm will not work.
But I don't have to worry about it
as my rival's incantation
wouldn't work either.

My anxiety when I meet her
is highly perplexing.
Is it the fear of the rival
that is forcing me
into this predicament?

Enjoyed her delightful company –
a rare divine blessing!
But in the sheer joy of the moment
I forgot to sacrifice my life.

I can imagine a scowl on her face
inside her veil.
But outside, there is simply a crease
in the fold.

Millions of flattering statements,
one stolen glance of her eye.
Millions of ornamentations,
one irate motion.

A lament that does not find place
in the beloved's heart
is equal to a straw.
It might otherwise be a lament
that causes a rupture in the sun.

A spell is not a spell
that doesn't fulfill my aspiration.
A spell is not a spell
even if it makes rowing possible
in a mirage.

Ghalib, I gave up booze.
But now and then I do relish my drink –
when the days are cloudy
and the moon shines brightly.

THE MYSTERY OF MYSTERIES

For the fear of the Day of Judgment,
don't give up on drinking today.
Imagine the disrespect to Saqi
of the river flowing in the paradise.

What has become of us humans?
Remember the time
when God asked the angels
to bow before Adam?

Our soul tends to soar
listening to the notes of a melody.
What we actually hear is His voice
in the musical instruments.

Life is like riding a horse
who will stop we don't know where.
We do not have our hands on the reins
or feet on the stirrups.

I'm as far away
from my own reality
as I'm from
solving the great mystery of life.

The one who is observing,
the one who is observed,
and the very act of observing
are all one and the same.
I wonder how to make sense
of what we are observing.

We know the ocean
by a variety of images it projects.
There is nothing much otherwise
if we view it as a drop of water,
a wave, or the sparkle.

She feigns shyness
by covering herself.
But strangely
the veil makes her appear
even more alluring.

She is not finished
beautifying herself.
From behind the veil
she is looking at the mirror.

The mystery of mysteries
that we witness
is a dream
for those who have been awakened
in their dreams.

Ghalib, His scent radiates
from the presence of His friend.
I am busy in my devotion
to Hazrat Ali.[35]

---

[35] Hazrat Ali, cousin and son-in-law of the Prophet. A revered figure in Shia Islam. He is also known by several nicknames: Father of Dust, Saqi of Kausar, and Asadullah (also Ghalib's first name).

WALKING WITH MY GUIDE

Given my fate
I do not know
whether I should lament
the loss of my heart
or my liver.
I wish I could hire
a professional mourner
to do this job
of crying for me.

I am ashamed to inquire
where your home is located.
In a confused state of mind,
I'm asking everyone I meet –
which direction should I take.

I had to look up
my rival's door a thousand times.
I wish I had not known
the paths you take
while you go about town.

I don't care
about the belt that you tie
around your waist.
Don't I know
the reality of your waist?

Lo, even she says
that I am naked
and without a name.
If I had known this

I would have been more careful
to not let my possessions
be plundered.

Though I'm able to walk
with those who walk really fast,
I still don't know
who is my guide and
where he is taking me.

Foolish see desire
as dedication.
Do I worship that idol
who is without a heart
or compassion?

In a rare case of forgetfulness
I forgot where she lived.
How miserable!
If I was self-aware
I would have certainly
gone there to find myself.

I guess other people in the world
are just like me – good at heart --
and using their skills
to do good work.

Ghalib,
I wish God bestows upon Ali Bahadur[36]
great honor.
I want to see this virtuous man
ride a horse with great pride.

---

36 Nawab Ali Bahadur was Ghalib's relative and a benefactor.

Part Five

My home is no different
from the one in the wilderness,
except that it is small in size.
Living in the luxury of wilderness
I forgot that I have a real home.

Ghalib loved natural beauty which he found in deserts and flowering gardens. *My Two Homes* [p. 191] gives expression to this yearning. For him the highest pleasure was going to the garden in the company of the beloved. This was a dream because the city in which he lived witnessed one calamity after another. Much of the greenery around Delhi was destroyed during the famine. The breakdown of law and order made it impossible for anyone to go to a natural habitat in the suburbs without armed escorts that only the very rich could afford. In these circumstances, a home in the wilderness is a dream for that part of self that wants to free itself from living in a home because it brought no happiness.

In the same ghazal, the poet wonders why the flowers have lost their color. Maybe nature is taking note of what was happening in the world that humans inhabited. The second question that embeds two powerful metaphors (flowers as colorful lamps and personification of wind) highlights the sense of loss: something that existed but is missing now.

Why has the color
of tulips and roses
faded away?

Aren't we missing
the colorful lamps
in the path of the wind?

The Decline Of The Natural World [p. 194] could be the result of extreme pessimism that the poet exhibited in a number of ghazals – a reflection of the feeling that the world around him was falling apart. Or was the poet predicting the future? Ghalib lived at the start of the industrial revolution, the invention of motor vehicles and related advances within decades of his death that changed the Man-Nature equation. Whatever way we look at the following couplet, it is a comment on the way things are today.

The natural world
is in decline
and is going to perish.
The sun is looking like a lamp
in the path of the tempest.

In *The Whirling Dance Of Flowers* [p. 197] the poet takes reification to an extreme with blooming flowers drinking deep colors and getting intoxicated. Then they dress loosely and dance like whirling dervishes.

The flowers bloom
intoxicated by their deep colors.
They wander dressed loosely
doing the whirling dance
of dervishes.

What Did We Miss? [p. 200] has two couplets that are a reflection on human interface with nature. The opening couplet in this ghazal makes us look at the soil of the earth with new eyes. We take it for granted that what we plant will show up as a sapling, a flower, a bush, or a tree. This gives us the feeling of being in charge. We command and the earth obeys. The poet shatters this myth. What we see is not entirely the outcome of our doing. There are things that sprout about which we know nothing. The poet's surprise has to do with things that come out and those that stay hidden. What stays hidden is nature's secret.

Roses and tulips rose
from under the ground.
But I was surprised
about the things that didn't sprout.
What images did we miss?
What did we not see?

Another couplet from the same ghazal shows the ease with which the poet is able to enter the natural world and become an indistinguishable part.

The garden became
a house of poetry
as soon as I entered.
Listening to my laments,
even the nightingales
started to sing the odes.

A DROP IN THE RIVER

She doesn't want to hear
anything about me.
Not even bad
or insulting words.
This puts my rival
in a bind
because he likes
to bad mouth me.

The invitation
to walk in the garden
shows my good fortune,
though the good news
about my planned murder
no one talks about.

The visible world is no bigger
than the expanse of the Creator.
People say it's true
but I don't believe it.

I'm like a drop
that is part of the ocean.
Declaring myself God
like Mansur[37] is easy
but that's not my choice.

---

[37] Mansoor Hussain who declared *anal haq* meaning "I am God" and was put to death.

The desire to pull down and destroy
is a matter of the past.
I've lost my strength.
My weak body doesn't allow me
to wage these love battles anymore.

When I tell her
that I would get her
on the Day of Judgment,
she reminds me with some vanity
that I shouldn't
take her for a houri.

If you wish to be cruel to me,
so be it.
What I don't want you to do
is to ignore me.

I long for the wine
refined in Jamshed's goblet.[38]
Sorry, it's not in my nature
to accept any wine
extracted from grapes.

Though Zahuri[39] and I are poets
of equal rank,
Ghalib, this fact
is not acknowledged in practice.
I'm not famous enough,
they tell me.

---

[38] Jamshed, Emperor of Persia, had a wine goblet in which he could see future events.

[39] Ghalib refers to a poet who was not recognized for his poetical talent when he was alive.

MY TWO HOMES

No complaint against inventing
new ways to be cruel.
Please go on doing
what you have been doing.
I want to be oppressed more.

Cheers for the love's labor
being spent in building
a new palace for Khusrao.
But it is not going to help Farhad
to gain a good reputation.

My home is no different
from the one in the wilderness,
except that it is small in size.
Living in the luxury of wilderness
I forgot that I have a real home.

Accidents are a way
of gaining experience.
Wise ones have been telling us.
When waves strike,
they are as good
as a thump by a teacher.

Sad that my faithfulness
doesn't get any recognition.
She thinks I've grown too weak
to complain about these things.

Why has the color
of tulips and roses
faded away?
Aren't we missing
the colorful lamps
in the path of the wind?

The flower-picker picks you
and tucks you in the basket
beside flowers.
It's good news for you,
O Nightingale,
that the bird-catcher
is off-duty today.

She affirms by saying no, no.
But the way she says it
makes it sound like
she wasn't given a mouth
at the time of her birth.

The paradise is no less
than your alley in its glitter.
It has the same layout
but it is less crowded.

How can you complain Ghalib,
about being impoverished?
Have you forgotten the indifference
of your friends before your exile?

BURN AND MELT

She gave me the two worlds
and she thought I was gratified.
But I was overcome by modesty
and didn't know
what more
I could have asked.

As the journey was tiring,
many dropped out
at every juncture
and just a few were left.
What could the miserable wrecks do
when they didn't know
where to find you?

Why do people
in the gathering
have no pity for the candle?
When the grief is
overwhelming,
there is little
that the pacifiers can do.

SUGARY TALK

My rival's sugary talk
has enamored her
and has snagged those
who really love her.

Poor fellows,
they know how to express
their love in silence
but not as a sweet talk.

A MEETING IN THE WILDERNESS

I told her
how Laila came to see Majnun,
indirectly suggesting
our meeting in the wilderness.
Surprised, she asked,
"Does it happen in this world?"

Ghalib, do feel compassion
for her tender heart,
and do not get her excited
about testing others' affections.
It may not do her any good.

THE DECLINE OF THE NATURAL WORLD

She developed liking
for sitting alone
after she fell in love.
My helplessness
got vindicated at last.

The natural world
is in decline
and is going to perish.
The sun is looking like a lamp
in the path of the tempest.

SHE CAME TO MY HOME

When I stare
at the walls and doors
of my home
during our separation,
I'm either looking for the fresh breeze
or just waiting for the carrier
to deliver your letter.

She came to my home
and I wondered about the miracle.
I looked at her
and then I looked at my home.

I don't want any harm done
to her hand and her arm.
Some people are looking
at my liver's deep wounds
and are trying to make a connection.

Why should I look at the jewels
of the brooch on your headdress?
I'm simply amazed
at the good luck
of the rubies and pearls.

HEART THAT CAN'T BE HAPPY

It is not
that I don't believe
in the Doomsday.
It is the belief
that the Day of Judgment
could not be worse
than the night of separation.

Will someone tell me
what is wrong
with moonlit nights?
I'm not concerned
whether the day is
breezy or cloudy.

No "nice to see you"
when I come face to face.
No "have a good day"
when I leave her company.

Even when she remembers me,
it's a rather strange way
to think of someone.
She says, "Why is there
no noise, disorder,
and chaos in the
gathering today?"

Wine is also available on days
other than the day of Eid.
Those who wait outside the tavern
are not disappointed.

Whether there is joy
or sorrow in the world,
it is not my concern.
God has given me
a heart that can't be happy.

Don't remind her Ghalib
that she ever made promises.
What's the use of saying it
when she will simply tell me,
"That one I don't remember."

THE WHIRLING DANCE OF FLOWERS

I write a poem
in praise of her light-footed horse
calling him a current of air.
It's another way for me
to inject some hot air
into my verse making.

No one has seen a sigh
to do any good.
I go on pushing my luck
nevertheless.

If I compare my life
with the life from its origin,
it is like asking how much time
henna will take to dry up
if we apply it on the lightening's feet.

I know how to find release
from the bondage of existence.
Yet I go on shedding tears
endlessly.

The flowers bloom
intoxicated by their deep colors.
They wander dressed loosely
doing the whirling dance
of dervishes.

Ask not
where my verse
might have gone wrong.
People tend to confuse
one's aspirations
with a binding commitment
of perfection.

O the foolish doings
of the wise ones!
They apply henna
on the blisters.

The one whom I love Ghalib
is artfully deceptive,
though she expects
a binding agreement of faithfulness
from me.

THE WORLD IS NOT TOO HARD ON ASAD

The world is really
not too hard on you Asad.
Or is it that my expectations
were just too high?

WHAT I'M NOT

You will not find me
lying on your doorsteps.
My life is shameful
but I'm not a stone.

Why shouldn't I get upset
by the constantly changing
nature of things?
I'm a human being,
not a goblet or a decanter.

O God, why do people
want to wipe me off.
I'm not like a letter written
on the world slate
twice as a mistake.

There ought to be a limit
to the harshness
of my punishment.
I'm a sinner
but not an infidel.

I don't know why
you don't treat me
as someone dear to you.
Ruby, emerald,
gold or pearl, I'm not.

Why do you refuse to keep
your feet on my eyes?
My status is no less
than that of moon or sun.

Why do you stop me
from kissing your feet?
Why do you think
I'm not equal to heaven?[40]

Ghalib,
as a pensioner of His Majesty's,
I do have to praise him.
Gone are the days
when I could say
that I was no one's servant.

WHAT DID WE MISS?

Roses and tulips rose
from under the ground.
But I was surprised
about the things that didn't sprout.

---

[40] There is a reference here to the belief that on the night of his final journey, the Prophet placed his feet in the direction of the heaven for a welcome kiss.

What images did we miss?
What did we not see?

I remember
the colorful beautifications
of her gatherings.
But now they are no more
than the carvings
in the domes of memory.

The constellations of seven stars –
the daughters of the dead in the sky –
are hiding behind the veil of the daylight.
God knows what came to them
that they bared themselves
in the dead of night.

Jacob didn't inquire about Joseph
when the latter was in the prison,
but his eyes stayed fixed at Joseph
as if they were prison's
window treatments.

Unhappy with Egyptian women
who had doubts about Joseph's beauty,
Zulekha was pleased in the end
hearing how they were stunned
by his good looks when they saw him.

In this night of separation,
let the blood flow from my eyes.
I will know that
two candles have been lit.

We shall exact retribution
from the fairies when we meet them
in the paradise
if by the grace of God
they are present there.

He is the lucky one
who sleeps calmly,
has the peace of mind,
and to whom all the nights belong.
He is the one on whose shoulders
you spread your tresses
promiscuously.

The garden became
a house of poetry
as soon as I entered.
Listening to my laments,
even the nightingales
started to sing the odes.

Her glances
go on piercing my heart O God,
though due to my bad luck
they were partially blocked
by her eyelashes.

Though I tried my best
to contain my sighs
inside my chest,
they continue to pour out
and even stitched the collar

that I had once torn
in a state of insanity.

Even if I showed up,
how would I deal
with her recriminations?
All the blessings that I knew
I showered on the doorkeeper.

Wine is life giving indeed.
Lines on the palm of the hand
become clear for the one who
holds the goblet.

I believe in one God
and my way of life
is to discard traditions and rituals.
Religious differences are harmful
when people do not believe
in the oneness of God.

Getting used to sorrow
alleviates the pain of sorrow.
Hardships don't bother me now.
They are so many
that they have become
easy to live by.

If Ghalib continued to shed tears
with the same intensity,
be aware people of the world,
all these places would be ruins.

A SELF-ASSESSMENT

My insanity has not spared
even a sacred thread on my body.
When I ripped my clothes,
nothing was left intact.
Not even one thread.

For her one glimpse
I sacrificed my heart.
But without the heart
I didn't have the strength
even to look at her.

Meeting you is not easy,
yet it's easy.
Otherwise, I would have given up
trying to see you.
The challenge is that
there is no challenge.

I can't lead my life without love.
Yet I don't even have the strength
to relish the rapture
that pain brings.

In this state of madness,
my head feels like a heavy burden
on my shoulders.
But what can I do in a desert?
There is no wall here
to strike my head against.

Leave aside the fight
that I should have with my rivals.
In a moment of weakness,
I have lost the lust for her company.

The fear of suffering in life is real.
Put your faith in God.
Even the rooster in the cage knows this.

In my heart are the tracings
of her eyelashes.
Yet I don't have the strength to suffer
the pain from a thorn.

Who would not kill oneself, O God,
on watching this aura of innocence.
She is engaged in a fierce fight,
but there is not even a sword in her hand.

Asad has been seen in public
and in the privacy of his home.
If he is not a certified lunatic,
he is not very smart either.

ONE THOUSAND HEARTS

There is not a single wound in my body
that a needle can stitch back to health.
Thread in the eye of the needle
is shedding tears of despondency.

I have no desire to see
how my home was ruined.
The foam created by the waters
of the flood
turned itself into balls of cotton
to plug leaks in the walls.

I have record of the excesses
of your eyelashes.
Just as each drop of my blood
has your name carved on it.

To whom can I narrate
the darkness
of my sleeping quarters?
Imagine a moonlit night
and someone has placed
cotton balls
into the openings in the walls.

My friends thankfully helped me
to overcome the worst part of frenzy.
Their laughter worked as a stitch
to repair my torn collar.

When her radiant beauty
reflected itself
on the mirror's surface,
the mirror coating broke
into tiny particles
that could be seen
floating in the air
as sunrays filtered
through the window.

I can't say I'm good or bad
because I'm sending
conflicting signals.
If I'm a flower
then I'll be thrown
into the waste basket.
If I'm a straw,
then I'm going to languish
in the garden.

The madness of love has given me
one thousand hearts.
Every drop of blood in my body
has turned itself into a black spot
of the shape of the heart.

Asad, I am a captive of my mad love.
The arches of her arms,
when she embraced me,
turned into a badge of slavery.

NOT EVEN DUST

Pleasures and joys
of the world
as they unfold
before my eyes
are not as good as dust.
Except for the blood flowing
in its veins,
the liver is dust,
not even dust.

If I turn into dust
by chance
then the wind
will carry me away.
My body,
weak as it is,
equals dust,
not even dust.

Beware!
The one
with heavenly nature
is coming.
Pathways
are embellished
with roses,
and nothing else
shows itself,
not even dust.

She was not expected
to care for me
but I should have shown
more compassion
for my own self.
My shallow breath
is dust,
not even dust.

The wine-lovers
are intoxicated
thinking of the beauty
of the flowers.
But on the walls and doors

of the tavern
there is nothing,
not even dust.

I have been shamed
by the destructive power
of love.
O my ambition
that is driving me
to rebuild my home.
Please listen!
There is nothing
to get the job done,
not even dust.

Asad,
my couplets
are good enough
for just one thing:
to please my heart.
It's now an open secret
that the use of my talent
for any other purpose --
not even dust.

WHY SHOULD I?

It's just a heart,
not a stone or a brick.
Being drowned in sorrow
is a natural thing.

I may cry a thousand times,
but why should anyone
badger me?

Neither a temple,
nor a mosque.
Neither a doorstep,
nor a threshold.
I'm just squatting
by the roadside.
Why should I be asked
to leave?

When her beauty
lights up hearts
like the afternoon sun,
and when she is the whole spectacle,
why does she hide her face
behind the veil?

Her amorous glances
strike an onlooker
like a dagger.
Although it is her own reflection
in the mirror,
she needs to exercise
some caution
lest it hurt her as well.

This bondage of life and
the unending flow of sorrow –
they are really one.
Why should a man

expect to be freed
from the grip of sorrow
before he dies?

She doesn't test
the sincerity of her lovers
because of her goodness.
I'm not telling her
to tryout my rival,
but shouldn't she care to know
who he really is?

While she is stuck in her arrogance,
and I'm attached
to my old style good manners,
I don't want to meet her
on a pathway,
and she doesn't wish to invite me
to her assembly.

Yes, she is not a believer.
She isn't even faithful.
If having faith
and good heart is dear to you,
why would you even
go to her alley?

Life goes on
without the help
of a dog-tired person like Ghalib.
We can cry bitterly
or let the world listen
to our wails and groans.

LIKE THIS

Don't parade an unopened flower
standing away from me and say
"like this."

Since I'm asking for a kiss,
you need to demonstrate with lips
"like this."

Stop complaining that she is a heart-stealer.
It is well-known without her saying a word.
Each of her pleasing statements and gestures say
"like this."

Late at night, drunk, in the company of my rival.
O God, please let her come to my place.
But on a second thought, dear God, maybe not
"like this."

When asked how was the night
that you spent in my rival's company,
she comes and sits in front of me and says
"like this."

Why shouldn't I stay quiet in her assembly?
The purpose of her silence is to say
"like this."

I told her that strangers had no place in her assembly.
She listened, that cruel distributor of pain, and
asked me to get up and leave
"like this."

She asked me what would make me lose my senses.
Seeing my predicament, the air started to blow fast
and said
    "like this."

I don't remember the code of conduct
for good behavior in her alley.
But the footprints mirrored my dilemma
and said
    "like this."

If you think that our union will result
in the decline of our desire for each other,
just look at the waves.
They are brushed aside by the ocean
but they keep coming
    "like this."

For those who say
how could Urdu ghazal be better
than the ones written in Persian,
just show them Ghalib's verse
    "like this."

THE GARDEN DUST

If your heart is overcome with jealousy,
then start looking around.
When you see more of what is happening,
your vision will broaden and
your thinking will expand
by watching things unfold.

My heart's longing and the propensity for sin
need to be balanced.
If my sins are equal to the waters in the seven seas,
they would hardly fill my lap.

If she comes to the garden,
looking tall and walking her flirtatious walk,
the garden dust will blow and sing
like ring-necked dove's mad melody.

A SLANTED-CUT PEN

If I have decided to settle in Kaaba,
it doesn't mean
that I would forget my connection
with my friends of the temple.

People pray to gain heaven's comforts
of wine and honey.
I say take the heaven and throw it into the hell.

I rebel against those who preach do good.
If the story of my life has been written
with a slanted-cut pen, why should I care?

Ghalib, please don't get too worked up
to make your own destiny.
Remember, the lightening will burn the harvest
if it hasn't already been eaten by the locusts.

A CURE FOR THE SORROW OF LOVE

It could just be that she loves me,
but maybe not.
I take this in a carefree manner
and want to keep it that way
even if there is bad blood between us.

Frailty has not left
any spark for love-making.
My heart is heavy
but it could be the stain of your love
weighing on my heart.

I do not like when you talk about my rival.
Whatever the motive,
I don't want to hear a thing about him.

Cure has been found, they say,
for every suffering.
That might be the case.
Why isn't there a cure
for the sorrow of love?

Being penniless prevented me
from dealing with others.
I should be embarrassed
but I'm not.

Man is a confused bundle
of scattered thoughts.
What is seen as fellowship
may very well be solitude.

Being influenced by others
when you're in a state of distress
is close to pitiful.
Don't take it even if it is a rebuke.

The freedom to act on one's own
is not an excuse
to detach self from the others.
One has to always seek from within
even if it means living in solitude.

The fear of moments dying
can't be fully erased.
It's our choice however
to spend the rest
of our precious life
simply praying.

Asad shall not leave her doorsteps,
though this action
will cause Doomsday disaster.
So be it!

LIKE A BIRD IN A CAGE

Like a bird I live in a cage
but the birds don't like my sad songs.
O singing birds of the garden,
why can't you empathize
with my loathsome life?

If I couldn't get the warmth of her love,
I could live with that.
But, O God, why did you give my rival
a passionate yearning for the one I love?

How sad that you didn't shed one tear
when you looked at my wound.
But the eyelashes of the needle
that was stitching the wound
were blood stained.

O God, you must punish my hands.
They either grab and pull my own collar
or they reach out to the edges of her dress.

In my simplicity,
I feel that I can see the killing field.
But what I haven't seen yet is
how your nimble horse
swims in the river of blood.

When I heard the news
that a chain is being built for my feet,
particles in the iron ore
still being mined
went into a chaotic swirl.

How could I be happy
when rain clouds are hovering
over my fields hundreds of time, and
when I know that lightning
has already set its eyes
on my crop.

I was robbed during the day
but it made me sleep easy
during the night.
Since robber stole everything,
I pray that his soul be blessed.

If I can write verses
like gems and jewels,
why should I go
in search of them elsewhere?
Digging stuff in the mines,
I don't have the stamina for that.

My Emperor, O Ghalib,
is more like Sulaiman.[41]
He is not simply a Faridun, Jam,
Kaikhusro, Darab, or Bahman.

ABOUT FEET

When I wash her ivory-textured feet
for a sip of honor and she pulls them back.
Hubris, arrogance, whatever you call it.

I gave my life away easily
and should kiss mountain-digger's feet.[42]

---

41 Ghalib wrote this couplet in praise of Emperor Bahadur Shah Zafar, for whom he served as a court poet. Hazrat Sulaiman, a legendary character, has the ability to fly. The second line refers to some well-known Persian kings.

42 Ghalib refers to Farhad, who was digging the canal for his beloved Shirin. The messenger was a man disguised as a woman to give him the false news that Shirin had died.

Alas, why didn't the messenger's feet break
before giving the news!

I got punished for running after her.
Now I'm in bondage thanks to the feet of someone
who ran away from me like a highway-robber.

I have traveled far and wide in search of a cure.
Though I'm tired,
my feet hurt more than anything else.

With Allah's grace,
my passion for wandering in the desert
survived my death.
Lo and behold,
my feet were moving inside the coffin.

The spring is at its peak
and flowers are in full bloom all around.
When the birds fly,
their feet are becoming entangled.

She may have appeared
in someone's dream last night.
Otherwise, how to explain the pain
in the iconic feet of her delicate body?

Ghalib, let there be great enjoyment
in my verse.
I'm blessed by the sweetness
of Khusro's poetic diction.[43]

---

[43] Hazrat Amir Khusro was a 13th century Sufi mystic and a poet who developed several forms of Hindi and Urdu poetry.

THE MIRROR

Over there, her heart is beating fast
and over here, I feel ashamed.
I'm afraid my sighs may have created
this situation.

Thanks to her vanity,
she doesn't look at herself in the mirror
unless the mirror itself
is the eye of her latest catch.

K IS FOR KINDNESS

I fainted repeatedly on reaching her alley.
Was it my intent to kiss the ground
under my feet a hundred times?

I keep my heart and my heart keeps me
filled with her love.
Both of us enjoy being willing captives.

Because of my physical weakness
I can't carry even the footprint
of an ant on my neck.
How can I gain the strength
to run away from her alley?

If you ignore me knowingly
then I can have some hope for reconciliation.
Your look that ignores me unknowingly
is a poison pill.

My cries very much sound like
the rooster's crowing.
People listen to him and not me.
It's a double-edged sword.

When I asked her to repeat her promise
to chop off my head, she smiled and said,
"I swear on your head not to do any such thing."

The reason
I wanted my heart to bleed
is to add
some luster to my eyes.

Your delicate nature takes my silence
as a cry for help.
I am so weak that I can't bear to see
your indifference.

Why did I come to Lucknow?
Not for sightseeing.
Certainly I don't have the appetite for that.

This city is not my destination.
I wanted to see Najaf
and the circle around Kaaba.

There is a hidden yearning
that is taking me places, Ghalib.
It is Almighty's Kindness
with a capital K!

WHEN TAVERN WAS TAKEN AWAY

If you want to be friends with my rival,
that's your choice, though it is not sinful
to ask about me from time to time.

Interrogation on the Day of Judgment
can't be avoided.
If my rival killed me, you are the only witness.

Do they also kill innocents and
take away the rights of others?
Admitting that you are not human
but a sun and a moon.

A thread is coming out of your veil.
I'm dying to know
whether it is someone else's glance.

When my tavern was taken away from me,
I was freed.
Now, it doesn't matter whether it is a mosque,
a school, or a monastery.

The praise for paradise is true.
But with God's grace it could also be the place
for your glorious manifestation.

When Ghalib is deceased, no one will miss anything.
But in God's name, I want the world to be there
and also my King!

Part Six

I'm ready to move
to a place
where there is no one around.
No one to share my melodies,
and no one who speaks
my language.

I want to build a home,
a home without doors and walls.
A home without a neighbor and
a home without a keeper.

If I fall sick
I want no one around
taking care of me.
And if I die
I want no one to mourn for me.

Dylan Thomas defined poetry as a "movement from an overclothed blindness to a naked vision." For Ghalib the naked vision was free and unadulterated expression of his thoughts and feelings. *A Home Without Doors And Walls* [p. 231] is a poem of three couplets that shows Ghalib in a gravely pessimistic mood. He often talks about living in "wilderness" but this one is different. It is about creating a living space that has some resemblance to a home as we conventionally know but not completely the same thing because the house has no doors or walls. The poet wants no one around, which is a definitive statement about complete social withdrawal. The reader is left asking the question as to what the people around him might have done to make the poet think of such a radical move. The poem depicts raw simplicity and is written in simple words that cry for attention.

Great poetry has words that demand recitation and beg to be converted into a musical score. This is especially true of Persian and Urdu ghazals that are rhymed in such a way that they can be easily arranged into musical arrangements and can be sung. A large number of Ghalib's ghazals have been sung by some of the great singers of our time. Whether or not you know the language is not material to enjoying a ghazal sung by a great artist. The music captures listener's attention and, before long, one is fully engrossed in the interplay of words and musical notes.

What makes Ghalib's ghazals so attractive to the musicians? *Let It Be* [p. 250] is an example of perfect synthesis of thoughts and words that require little effort to be converted into a song. Here is the opening couplet in original Urdu:

Ishq mujh ko nahin, vahshat hi sahi
Meri vahshat, teri shohrut hi sahi

The free verse translation reads:

I'm more in love with wilderness
than with you.
My wandering brings you
unwanted fame and attention.
Let it be.

We note several things at first glance. Ghalib says something in two lines of 8 syllables each that is difficult to translate with the same precision and emotional intensity in English. Second, the poet uses several poetical techniques to enhance the musical potential of this ghazal. For example:

> *Assonance:* vowel sounds to create internal
> rhyming within couplets.
> *Repetition:* the poet follows the rulebook of ghazal writing
> that requires a certain pattern of rhyming and repetition.
> *Alliteration:* the repetition of consonant sounds.
> *Consonance:* several words sounding together

This ghazal is also remarkable for its description of particular states of consciousness. Wilderness is not only a physical space, it is also a psychological state of a frustrated lover. Hatred, for instance, could form the basis of a relationship. Awareness could be deemed ignorance. Obliviousness as a state of mind could lead to a behavior that knowingly inflicts pain on the lover.

WHAT WOULD MAKE IT HAPPEN

There was a time
when I imagined:
there must be a different way to talk with you.
Better communication, not just words?
    What would make it happen?

In my imagination
I think of only one thing: union.
Union with the beloved?
    What would make it happen?

It is my respectful demeanor
that stops me from sharing my dilemma.
Being more forthright?
    What would make it happen?

Tell me what should the lovers and
idolators do with their lives
Some sympathy for the lovers?
    What would make it happen?

Seeing the image in the mirror,
you get agitated.
There are more like you.
Less indignation?
    What would make it happen?

Gloomy days like mine,
you will not know day from the night.
Less gloominess?
    What would make it happen?

With my help, you can start
to value my friendship
and things can change.
Making you aware of my state of mind?
    What would make it happen?

I felt good when I read your letter,
but my eyes weren't too pleased.
Meeting you face to face?
    What would make it happen?

How can I have peace of mind
looking at your eyelashes?
Making your eyelashes less sharp?
    What would make it happen?

Madness has not vanquished Ghalib
but the Emperor has rightly said.
"Consolation in the time of separation
from the beloved?
    What would make it happen?"[44]

---

[44] The second line of this couplet is drawn from a ghazal written by Emperor Bahadur Shah Zafar.

IF YOU ARE SOMEONE'S FRIEND

Why complain
when you have willingly
given away your heart?
When the heart is gone,
how could words
come out of the mouth?

If she is unwilling
to give up haughtiness,
why should I change my style?
Is it frivolous for me to ask:
why was she upset with me?

My well-wisher has added
to my notoriety.
To hell with such sympathy!
He does not understand my sorrow;
he is not qualified to be my confidant.

What faithfulness?
What love?
I'm just smashing my head.
Then, why my stonehearted beauty,
shouldn't this be your threshold?

While I'm imprisoned
don't share with me, my friend,
the story of my colorful habitat.
Where the lightening struck yesterday,
I hope, was not my abode.

You can say
"I am not in your heart,"
but then explain this to me.
When you are the only one in my heart,
why are you not visible to me?

It is wrong to complain
about the heart's passion.
Whose fault is this?
Tension between us will end
when you stop moving
away from me.

Is love simply not good enough
to wreck a man's life?
If you are someone's friend,
why would the sky be his enemy?

You are testing me.
In reality, it feels
you're poking fun at me.
When you have banded with my rival,
what is left to test me?

You asked, "Is my meeting
with your rival a matter of
concern to you?"
You're right.
You speak the truth.
Say it again.
Why should it be?

What are you trying to achieve Ghalib
with your jibes?
When you call her unkind
that does not make her benevolent.

A HOME WITHOUT DOORS AND WALLS

I'm ready to move
to a place
where there is no one around.
No one to share my melodies,
and no one who speaks
my language.

I want to build a home,
a home without doors and walls.
A home without a neighbor and
a home without a keeper.

If I fall sick
I want no one around
taking care of me.
And if I die
I want no one to mourn for me.

MIRRORS LOOKING AT ONE ANOTHER

From the sun to the particles,
heart is seen in every mirror.
A parrot looks around
and finds mirrors
looking at one another.[45]

SPRING AND AUTUMN

There is grass growing
on every nook and cranny of my deserted home.
If this is spring's doing, please do not ask me
about the autumn.

Accept the frustrations that life brings and
please do not ask –
the journey's hardships and the blows
you get from the fellow travelers.

STONES AS THE CURRENCY

His glories are seen face to face
if we just lift our eyelashes.
But there is no strength

45 This verse lends itself to different interpretations. Heart is a symbol of humanness and love. It is the only binding force in the universe. Parrot acting as an onlooker has the capacity to appreciate the power of love from a non-human perspective.

to unravel the mystery
behind the vision.

Love-lunatics have to accept
stones as their currency.
Their reward is
what the children are throwing
at them.

The wall bends itself
to show its gratitude
to the mason.
But if your home was ruined,
you don't owe anything
to anyone.

Either stop talking
about my wounds
coming from jealousy,
or lift the veil that hides
your beautiful smile.

MOSQUE AND THE TAVERN

We need a tavern
under the shadow of the mosque.
Just like eyes need the brow.
We need it, O God!

Since you have fallen in love
with the other, you will know
what it means to suffer in love.

Praise, O Heaven, the heart
that has suffered the pangs of love!
There ought to be redress
for the wrongs done in the past.

I have learned to paint
for the sake of
those moon-like beauties.
After all, you need an excuse and
an occasion to meet them.

Unless you are disgraced,
you will have nothing to do
with drinking.
What I seek
is a state of unconscious bliss
every night and day.

The color of flowers
such as tulips and roses
is different.
But in every color and shade
there is an affirmation of spring.

When it is time to enjoy,
we should bury our head
under the decanter.
When it is time to pray,
we should turn our face toward Kaaba.

They watch the rotation of the cup
filled with wine.
Those who know the secret
are roaring drunk.

Our growth in reality, Ghalib,
radiates from our roots.
The words we cherish
emanate from our silence.

TUMBLERS UPSIDE DOWN

My humble heart is reduced
to a drop of blood.
With its head lowered,
it is ready to drip what's left.

I was annoyed
with that lustrous beauty
in my own way.
Decorum aside,
it was a distinctive expression
of my madness.

The thought of death
can provide little comfort
to the wounded heart.
In the snare of my desires,
death is certainly
a very weak catch.

I would not have cried
had I known my dear friend
that this itself would become
the source of great suffering.

Be not so proud
of the sharpness of your sword.
It is just a wave of blood
in the river of my impatience.

Why ask the Saqi in the sky
for the luxurious vintage wines.
She is sitting uptight
with multiple tumblers upside down.

My heart longs for union Ghalib,
and to quibble about separation.
May God bring that day
when I am able to tell her
about this and that.

THE MOVING DECANTER

In the company of idols,
my lips are sealed.
Fed up with useless fawning
and adulation.

The moving decanter
is a source of some frustration.
Just bring it to my lips and
let me drink in one gulp.

Those at tavern's door
are not worthy of your time,
O Preacher.
Beware of these rowdies
because they lack good manners.

Seeing how bad things happen
to loyal lovers, my soul left,
though she briefly sat on my lips
before her final departure.

NO PROMISE

So that I am left
with no ground to complain,
she listens to me.
But she doesn't talk about me,
and doesn't mention my name.

Ghalib, we shall communicate
what's going on right now.
Whether she will call you
on hearing the news,
we can't promise.

THE DESIRE TO REBUILD

There was nothing
in my home
that my longing for you
would have destroyed.
The desire to rebuild
the foundation
of a broken heart
though still remains.

A FLAME INSIDE A SILK FABRIC

If I get a chance
to think of something else
other than the woes of the world,
then looking at the sky
would be enough
to bring your memory back to me.

How would she know
the contents of my letter to her, O God?
That kafir has taken a vow
and is determined to burn the paper.

The flame can hide
inside a silk fabric
though it is hard to believe.
But to hide the flame
burning in my tender heart
is another matter.

She really wanted
to see her wounded victims.
A walk in the garden
was her flirty excuse.

It was my innocence
that killed me while seeing
your stylish gestures.
Your arrival, O Tyrant,
was nothing but a prelude
to your leaving.

I have little patience
left to be buffeted by the life's
ups and downs.
There was a time
when my strength assured my doing
idols' bidding.

Ghalib, what should I say
about the tradition of doing good
in this world.
The one who benefitted
turned out to be the one
who harmed me most.

A BLEMISH OF INCOMPLETENESS

Wash away the hope
of a bargain from your mind,
O Wishful Thinker!
The heart is already a
sunken commodity
floating in the pool of tears.

Like the candle
that has been forcibly extinguished
by someone,
I am burned too,
just carrying a blemish
of incompleteness.

AN ANT'S EGG

How cramped is the world
of the oppressed!
With sky no bigger
than an ant's egg.

The universe is in constant motion
yearning for You.
The smallest particle has life
because of the sun's rays.

It is rose-red because it has been struck
time and again.
People have funny ideas
that I am carrying red wine in my heart.

She is warming the hearts of the one
in the lascivious crowd.
Wonder why she likes abodes
that are cold.

It was nice that you didn't let
my rival kiss you.
Let us stay quiet about it
because I too have a tongue.

The person who loosens up
in the company of his beloved
will be idolized
as the person who rules
over as large a country as India.

Constant suffering has killed faith
in my life's purpose.
The scar is in the place
where my liver used to be.

Ghalib, I have put my trust
in her loyalty so much so
that even her lack of generosity
appears to be a source of happiness.

ALAS! ALAS!

My pain is making you restless.
Alas! Alas!
What happened to your obliviousness,
dear oppressor?
    Alas! Alas!

If your heart was not strong enough
to bear the pain of suffering,
why did you try to console me?
    Alas! Alas!

How did you get this idea
that you could console me?
The friendship with me
was enmity in your mind.
    Alas! Alas!

You gave me a vow of love for this life.
So what?
Life itself is not stable and permanent.
    Alas! Alas!

The tenor of my life was like a poison to me.
Meaning, it had a squabble with you.
    Alas! Alas!

Whatever happened
to the seductive mushrooming
of flowers?
Your flowers are now sprouting in the dust.
    Alas! Alas!

Afraid of being defamed,
you cover yourself in a veil of dust.
Concealment of love ends with you.
    Alas! Alas!

Our vows of love are now part of the dust.
The world is without love and friendship.
    Alas! Alas!

The hand that carried the sword became worthless.
My heart did not suffer a wound.
    Alas! Alas!

How to spend the night
when it continuously rains?
My eyes are used to looking at the stars.
    Alas! Alas!

My ears cannot hear your voice and
my eyes cannot see your beauty.
There is only one heart,
full of pain and suffering.
    Alas! Alas!

My love had not yet taken the color
of lunacy, Ghalib.
What was left in the heart
was a desire to be disgraced.
    Alas! Alas!

A VAGABOND HEART

With my madness increasing each day,
there is little hope of my survival.
The good news for my satisfaction --
death is on its way.

She no longer makes inquiries
about the fate of my vagabond heart.
I still own the thing.
Is that what she thinks?

For how long,
should I continue to rant and rave
about the ecstasy of my fevered body.
Each hair on my body
has gained a voice and is saying,
"Thank You."

The sheer arrogance
of being so beautiful
has made her faithless.
Otherwise, how could I explain
her behavior knowing that
she has her heart in the right place.

The moonlit night made me drink
all there was to drink.
My phlegmatic body
likes the warmth
that comes with drinking.

Asad, every home earns its identity
from its occupant.
After Majnun's death,
the forest is sad.

THE CURTAIN AND THE MIRROR

I can hide the real condition
of my heart
by not saying anything.
I'm happy
that no one understands
what I am saying.

To whom should I relate
the story of my choked up desires
and aspirations.
My heart can speak
but its voice is jumbled and confused.

O God!
Behind which curtain is your mirror image.
I beg your mercy.
I'm not questioning Your existence.
I just want to see You!

Shame on me
for entertaining this thought!
For God's sake,
why did I talk about your enmity?
My out of control desire,
what were you really thinking?

The cloth that covers Kaaba
has the fragrance of musk
because Ali was born there.[46]
It is the center of the earth and
not the center of a deer's navel.

The earth was rather small
for my frenzied wanderings.
The river's water
was sweat of embarrassment,
nothing much to talk about.

Asad, don't get trapped
in the deception of existence.
This world is a trap
built around the mesh
of our own thinking.

46 Hazrat Ali, the Prophet's son-in-law and cousin.

THE FIRE UNDERNEATH

Don't dig deeper and
try to probe my lamentations.
Watch out for my heart,
there is a fire buried underneath.

O Heart!
Your sorrow is a blessing in disguise.
In the end, there will be nothing.
No cries of the morning and
no sighs of the night!

THE DRUNKEN DANCE

Your hand had scribbled the word
"faithfully" in your letter
but that got erased.
The paper you selected to write the letter
had the ability to auto-erase
misleading statements.

Why is my heart burning
on its inability to extinguish itself?
There is something unique about me.
I do not burn down completely
though my breath is emitting fire.

When you throw water on the burning fire
its wailing cries rise up.
Everything moans to express its sadness
and helplessness.

He is the reason that every particle in the universe
is doing this drunken dance.
The ecstasy rising from the earth to the sky
is a manifestation of His being.

Don't say:
"You used to tell me that I was your life."
Let us not talk of my life.
I am dismayed with my life, to say the least.

At the start of my letter
you will see the drawing of an eye
so that you know how bad
is my longing to see you.

PALANQUIN

When she passes through my alley
in her palanquin,
she is in such great hurry
that she would not even let the bearers
shift the burden in their shoulders.

CAGE, FEATHERS, AND WINGS

My world has the ambience
of many stunning desires.
When you hear my moans,
what you hear is the sound
of an imaginary bird.

What is autumn?
What do you call spring?
Be it any season.
It is the same cage
and the same laments
about feathers and wings.

The kindness of the beloved
may be coincidental, my friend.
Who has ever seen the cries and
moans of a sad heart change
anything?

Though I was disappointed,
I did not have the feeling
of having been crushed.
When I wringed my hands,
it was a vow renewed to
meet the challenge.

THE SMOKE OF A BURNED OUT LAMP

Show some mercy,
dear oppressor.
What is the life of the smoke
of a burned out lamp?
The pulse of a patient of true love
is just like the smoke of a
burned out lamp.

The fact that I gave my heart to someone
keeps me restive and restless.
The lack of activity around me
has the feel of smoke of a
burned out lamp.

A WELCOME CARPET

The eyes of the beloved
speak in their silence.
Antimony in her eyes
is showing up
as the smoke of the flame
of her voice.

Lovers sound
like discordant
musical instruments.
Their moans
have the sound
of planets in motion.

Looking at Majnun's eyes
bathed in blood,
flowers sprouted in an instant
to make a welcome carpet.

LET IT BE

I'm more in love with wilderness
than with you.
My wandering brings you
unwanted fame and attention.
    Let it be.

Do not cut off with me.
If nothing else, let there be animus.
Hatred is also a relationship.
    Let it be.

What is the shame in my presence?
If it is not a public gathering,
it will be a private meeting.
    Let it be.

I'm not my own enemy,
but my life depends on your love.
I know that my rival loves you too,
but his life does not depend
on your love.
    Let it be.

We are, what we are, because we exist.
If there is no awareness,
forgetfulness prevails.
    Let it be.

Life is like rapid lightening.
This I know for sure.
There is enough time to bleed my heart.
    Let it be.

I'm never going to stop loving you.
If you don't return my love,
there will be calamity and ruin.
    Let it be.

O Unjust Heaven!
You have to give me something
at least.
Give me the freedom
to send you my moans and cries.
    Let it be.

I will gradually learn from you
the habit of obliviousness
that you have perfected.
    Let it be.

Asad, a little bit of flirting
is always fun among friends.
If there is no union,
there will be longing for union.
    Let it be.

A SINGER WITH A FIERY BREATH

My passion to wander
invites insults that I can live with.
Morning in my homeland
appears to show me its teeth
as if it is poking fun at me.

I am looking for a singer
whose singing reveals his
fiery breath.
I want his voice to hit me
with a force of lightening
to annihilate me.

As I traverse the valley
of my own thoughts
I am in a state of sheer ecstasy.
I am not concerned
with the echoes of my thoughts
or anything else.

The way you expose yourself
in the garden is far from modest.
I am ashamed
by the way the flowers start
to smell.

No one could ever know anything
about the affairs of my heart.
It is the selection of couplets
that has gotten me in trouble.

Part Seven

Ghalib, the manner in which
I have lived my life
makes me feel
that I had no God taking care of me.

Ghalib had a complex relationship with God. *An Autobiography In A Couplet* [p. 257] says it all in few words that are direct but hide the pain suffered over a lifetime. While on the one hand he was a strong believer, on the other he was troubled by the circumstances of his life. The people around him and the city where he lived made it challenging for him to accept the fact that there was a higher force committed to serving the public good.

As a nature lover, Ghalib was fascinated by the earth's potential to produce colorful flowers and food for the sustenance of life. But he also noticed that the earth often acted like a despot. People looked forward to seeing tulips and roses when they planted the bulbs or saplings, but what they actually got was flowers surrounded by weed and empty spaces. Earth gives the appearance of often acting like a miser, taking in more than it gave back.

In *A Question For The Soil* [p. 257], Ghalib asks about the fate of the people who were buried. They were "priceless treasures" because while they were alive they had creativity and spiritual prowess that made angels jealous. But when they died, they were nothing more than a clump of bones and the earth gladly took them in. The way Ghalib poses this question may have the appearance of dramatic inquiry for making the couplet more interesting to read but at its core it leads us to philosophical questions like: What is the real worth of life if in the end it is nothing more than the food for the soil? Will those people whose identity is now mixed with the soil ever rise and walk again?

If I am lucky, I would get a chance
to ask the soil, O Penny-pincher,
what did you do
with those invaluable gems
that we buried?

Ghalib had the knack for putting two unrelated ideas together and in their blending he created the ground for novelty—something that negated the original premise. Take for example a couplet from *Layers Of Feathers* [p. 261]. Ghalib looked at the universe and saw "singularity"—the quality of oneness, unity of form and function at its very best. This thought was immediately negated by its opposite: if everything was one, then why did he seek divine presence in one particle after another? This inner tension led him to a new insight: he sought the sacred in every particle because he was an idolator. Being an idolator confirmed the poet's identity as a lover since the beloved was always an idol, an object of veneration for the lover. Second, being an idolator made him an unconventional Muslim, a rebel, a religious pariah.

The whole universe is a proof of singularity.
My effort to see Him in each and every thing
has turned me into an idolator.

Rising from the sleep, Sufis tell us, is the awakening that connects us to our spiritual and evolutionary impulse. The following couplet from *Where Is Your Youth* [p. 264] reminds us of a recurring theme in Rumi's ecstatic poetry.

Where are those nights
when we drank ourselves into a stupor?
Rise and find your way
as the delights of the morning sleep
have come to an end.

AN AUTOBIOGRAPHY IN A COUPLET

Ghalib, the manner in which
I have lived my life
makes me feel
that I had no God taking care of me.

A QUESTION FOR THE SOIL

In order to stay in her company
I had to get rid of any sense of shame.
I continued to sit there
though there were indications
for me to leave.

It is just my heart.
Why was it petrified
by the doorkeeper's double-dealing?
How could I pass by your door
without calling your name?

In my frenzied state
I have pledged my rags and mats
to raise some cash.
It has been a long time
since I celebrated the spring's feast.

Life passes away without much getting done,
even if it is the life of someone like Khizr.
Even you, Sir, will ask: What did I do?

If I am lucky, I would get a chance
to ask the soil, O Penny-pincher,
what did you do
with those invaluable gems
that we buried?

There was no day
when the rival didn't try to pin
the blame on me.
There was no day
when he didn't use his tools
to saw off my head.

You probably got this bad habit
from my rival's company.
You kissed me
when I had not asked for it.

A bit stubborn,
but her habits are not bad.
In her forgetfulness,
she has met all her promises.

Ghalib, tell me what response would you get?
Granted that you would tell your story
and she would hear patiently.

THE SIX DIRECTIONS

The speed at which
life is passing through its tumultuous route,
one year can be measured
by the time it takes for the lightening to strike.

The cypress tree is acting
like a decanter filled with the spring wine.
The clouds are moving like one wave of wine
after another.

The crust of my determination
has been badly lacerated.
Neither have I the motivation to run away,
nor the vigor to stay behind.

In all the six directions
are spread the domains of wine lovers.
The ignorant suspect that there is something
wrong with the world.

How can I look straight at her electrifying beauty?
She hides her grandeur behind the veil
of a flowering spring.

Being the lover who lost,
I don't know how I could
comfort my heart.
Isn't it enough that my eyes
can still look at your face?

Asad, I am ready to forego
the pleasure of getting her letters.

I'm jealous of the communications
that the messenger is having
and what they are talking about me.

THE CANVAS GETS FLIRTATIOUS

Look at my luck!
I have become envious of myself looking at her.
How should I look at her?
I simply can't see anything.

The heart melts if it is caught up
in the heat of suspicion.
The flask melts if the wine is stiff.

How can she, O God,
stop a stranger from misbehaving,
when she is shy and
appears to be timid and hesitant.

Desire is addicted to complaining and
it is showing its discontentment
but my heart is in a feeble state
and it can hardly breathe.

I want evil eyes to stay away
from her joyous congregation.
My wailing turns into a melody
on reaching there.

She doesn't pay attention
to the secrets of our love

in her forgetfulness.
But when I appear lost
she makes some good guesses.

When I heard stories
of riotous celebration in her party,
my heart sank with sadness.
It seems the rival is succeeding
in making a deep impression on her.

That fairy-face became even more delicate
after she fell in love.
The color of her skin brightened
as she learned to fly.

As the artist gets ready to paint her,
the canvas gets flirtatious.
As he pulls it towards himself,
it pulls itself away.

Asad, my shadow is running away
from me like smoke.
Who can stay close to someone
whose soul is on fire?

LAYERS OF FEATHERS

Your delightful image on my bedspread
kept me warm.
This is how I saved myself
during the nights of our separation.

Knowing how even promises for salvation
in the other world are sold,
it was my fortitude that saved me
from these transactions.

The whole universe is a proof of singularity.
My effort to see Him in each and every thing
has turned me into an idolator.

I didn't lust for flowers
even in my imagination.
The loss of my own feathers
surprisingly
has given me strange comfort.

THE PAIN OF IMPATIENCE

Like everything else in the world,
tulip is marked for extinction.
When the farmer raises the crop
with his blood and toil,
lightening gets ready to strike.

Before blooming the bud feels secure,
though in its heart it knows
that its dream of becoming a flower
will soon be shattered.

How can I bear the pain of impatience?
The inner flame is giving up
by carrying straw in its teeth.

THE SPRING HAS ARRIVED

The walls of my home
are green with lush growth, Ghalib.
While I am roaming in the wilderness,
the spring has arrived at my home.

TALK ABOUT ME IN MY ABSENCE

My heart longs to die for her innocence.
I can't help it but the knife
is once again in the grip of the slayer.

Because of the terrific nature
of how she put into the words,
I felt that whatever she said
was already in my heart.

Although it comes up
with much blame and ridicule,
casual talk about me
in your gathering
is better than being there.

Enough, the crowd of despair,
all will go to ashes.
Everything –
including what we find
most satisfying
in our futile efforts.

Why even try
when the fatigue has fallen in love
with my feet?
Although I have the right path
to reach the destination,
I cannot move.

My heart is showing
leaping flames of hell.
But just ask yourself,
who has sparked the intensity
of this Doomsday scenario?

Ghalib, my heart is caught up
in suspicion and indecision.
Just be kind to my longing
because it is in a tough situation.

WHERE IS YOUR YOUTH?

Your one glance traveled
from my heart to my liver.
You won them over
with just one flirtatious move.

My chest is torn and
now I can enjoy carefree life.
Gone is the need to hide
the wounds of the heart.

Where are those nights
when we drank ourselves

into a stupor?
Rise and find your way
as the thrills
of the morning slumber
have come to an end.

The wind is blowing my ashes
in her alley.
Thanks O Dear Breeze!
The lust of tresses and feathers
to freely fly
has come to an end.

The style of her footprint
steals the heart.
She made waves
as the flowers got crushed.

Since freaks and deviants
have started exalting beauty,
there is no respect left
for those who love
from the heart.

The unmasking
of your beauty
surprised everyone
by serving as a veil.
Every intoxicated eye
that reached your face
got refracted.

The difference between
yesterday and tomorrow

was shattered.
When you left yesterday,
I had the experience
of the Doomsday.

The times and the people
have taken a toll on you
Asad Ullah Khan.
Where is your passionate robustness
and where is your youth?

A NEIGHBORHOOD WATCH

I will not ask for any consolation
if my passion to see you is fulfilled
by finding someone like you
in the maidens of the paradise.

Don't bury me in your alley
after you have killed me.
I don't want the world to know
where you live
from my final resting place.

Be respectful of your persona,
O Saqi.
I keep drinking each evening
all the wine I can get.

I have nothing to say to you,
my friend.

Convey my greetings to my courier
if you meet him.

I can demonstrate
what Majnun actually did.
But for that to happen
I have to get time off
from my hidden miseries.

It is not necessary
to follow in Khizr's footsteps.
I got to know him
as an elderly fellow traveler
in my life's journey.

O residents
of my beloved's alley,
I am asking you to keep a watch
if you ever find
that lunatic named Ghalib
in your neighborhood.

THE DAY OF MY FINAL DEPARTURE

My life is nearing its end.
But I'm not giving up.
A new intent
is blossoming inside.

The hell-fires
have no heat left in them.
But I can't say the same

about the flames of sorrow
that are slowly burning me
from the inside.

I have seen her annoyance
and irritation many a time.
But now, the intensity
of her indignation is something
that I've never seen.

The courier gives me your letter
and then looks at me.
I think there is something
that he has to say orally.

Stars do intervene
and cut short our lives.
But the heavenly calamity
is different
than what we go through
each day.

Ghalib,
I have lived through
many cataclysmic tribulations.
There is only one thing more --
the day of my final departure.

THE FIXED DAY

I don't see any hope.
Nothing is fulfilled and
hopelessness reigns.
I don't see a way out.

The day we die is fixed.
That being so…
Why can't I sleep at night?

I used to laugh
at the state of my heart.
Now, I can't laugh
at anything.

I know prayer helps.
So does piousness.
But these are not the things
that really attract me.

There is a reason
that I am silent.
Otherwise, I know
how to talk
convincingly.

Why shouldn't I howl
knowing that
she is thinking of me.
But unfortunately
my voice does not reach her.

The wounds of my heart
are not visible.
But O my caretaker,
why can't you smell them?

What a place have I reached
in my state of desolation.
I'm not getting any news
about my own self.

I die for the wish of dying.
Death comes
but it still doesn't come.

With what face
will you go to Kaaba, Ghalib?
Are you not ashamed?

MY MOST GULLIBLE HEART

My most gullible heart,
what's wrong with you?
There are remedies
for ailing hearts
but I don't know
the remedy for you.

I'm enthusiastic,
but she is disengaged.
O God!
I don't understand
what's going on here.

I too have a tongue
in my mouth.
I wish you could ask me
what I want.

When this world
doesn't exist without You,
then, O God, what is this
hullabaloo about?

What are these beauties
looking like fairies?
How do you describe
their flirtatious demeanor?

Why are there curls
in her fragrant tresses?
What is the meaning
of fashionably blackened eyes?

Tell me the source
from where these flowers
and greenery came?
What are these clouds made of?
What is the air that we breathe?

I expect fidelity
from someone
who doesn't even understand
what that means.

If you do good deeds
you will be rewarded.
What more a dervish could say!

I offer my life to you.
I don't know much about
the blessings of the prayer.

Agreed, Ghalib,
that it doesn't have much value.
But whatever it is –
if it is free, then just take it.

SHOCK AND SURPRISE

All of you are telling me
that the idol
with perfumed tresses
is coming to see me.
Just for a change --
show your shock and surprise
on her coming!

I'm in the throes of death and dying.
O my love's desire!
Though I can't speak,
I want her to come and see me,
simply asking about my well-being.

It's like the lightening hitting and
the flames of mercury rising
I don't understand
why I came to this world,
though I have a feeling that I do.

Angels will be seen running away
if they smelled from my mouth
traces of last night's wine.

No fear of the hangman and
no argument with the preacher.
I know them both;
no matter what garb they wear.

O seeker of truth!
You don't want to hear

the taunts of the people
about not finding Him?
You can't find Him
by looking around
though there is a good chance
that you might lose yourself
in the process.

It is not my habit to sit calmly,
simply doing nothing.
Since no one answered my call,
I went away and visited Kaaba.

I put more effort into my crying
at the suggestion of my friends.
They earned her goodwill, for sure,
but I was pushed deeper into sorrow.

Ghalib, what can I say
about her enchanting gathering.
I too went there
and cried my heart out
as my fate had decreed.

ONCE AGAIN

Once again,
my heart is in commotion.
And my chest is inviting
deeper wounds.

Once again,
my nails have started
digging into my liver.
Welcome to the season
when tulips blossom!

Eyes look for
what they desire to see.
But, once again, there is a veil
around the canopy.

The speed at which
my tears are flowing,
they are turning themselves
into a commodity.
My heart is a buyer
adding to my denigration.

Hundreds of ways –
same cries and laments.
Hundreds of times –
unstoppable shedding of tears.

The heart is yearning once again
to see her walk in style.
The commotion is very much like
people assembling for resurrection.

The beauty is once again
ready to display its charms.
It is the day when the lovers
have to be ready to die.

I still long for
my unfaithful beloved.
She is my life
again and again.

The doors to the court of beauty and
glamor are once again open.
The judge is looking at the plaints
of those with broken hearts.

The world is enveloped
in a veil of darkness.
Once again,
your tresses are in command.

Once again,
the shreds of my liver posed a question.
It's a cry for help.
There is lament and sorrow.

Once again,
lovers have been called as a witness.
They have been ordered to shed more tears.

The litigation between the heart and
the eyelashes is coming up once again
for hearing in the court today.

Ghalib, this state of rapture
is not without a cause.
There is certainly something that
she is hiding from me.

STONES, SPARKS, AND FLOWERS

Madness is not seeking any satisfaction
when it is in a celebratory mood.
The joys of life deep down
sprinkle salt on the heart's wounds.

How can we free ourselves
from the strivings of life?
The waves of water,
while flowing effortlessly,
become the chains.

My grave is a place that
kids love to visit.
But now, stones turn into
sparks of beautiful flowers.

THE DAGGER-TIPPED DESERT

Get ready to receive the retribution
if you complained against
your beloved's excesses.
The morning on the Day of Judgment
will hopefully show its teeth in laughter.

Let the dust of Majnun's desert
impart relief to Laila's veins.
Imagine if the farmers sowed

tips of daggers instead of seeds.[47]

Wings of the moth
perhaps became the sails
for the boat of wine.
This was enough
to warm up the party.

How should I narrate
my strong discomfort
to flutter my feathers.
The strength of the main wing
was lost even before taking off.

For how long I should go on crying
under the shadow of her tent.
It feels like Doomsday!
O God, was it too much for me
to expect a stone wall?

TRANSFORMED INTO SORROW

My excesses
brought me disrespect.
The more I crossed the limits,
the lesser was I as a person.

[47] A reference here to the Laila-Majun love story. When Laila slashed her veins, Majnun started to bleed as well. If farmers sowed daggers, Majnun will be hurt badly and consequently Laila will feel the pain.

The net was concealed
close to the nest.
I was easily trapped
as I started to fly.

Our existence is a proof
of our nonexistence.
I was diminished to a point
where I became
an excuse for myself.

Do not ask about them
who suffered
tribulations of love.
Slowly and gradually,
from head to toe,
they were transformed
into grief.

Your faithfulness
will not be the remedy
for what is wrong
with this world.
It was not only you,
there were others
who acted cruelly.

I continued to write
the blood dripping stories
of my craziness.
It is another matter
that in this process
I lost my hands.

Your short temper,
made my heart
to devour my cries and
my heart itself was gobbled
by the fire of my cries.

The victory of those
who are passionate
rests in their giving up the battle.
Running away from the field
is like a triumph for them.

I was given a finite number
of complaints in heaven.
What I could not use over there
were turned into breath here.

Even while panhandling,
Asad did not give up
his meditative style.
After becoming a beggar,
he fell in love with the generous.

THE GIFT OF PAIN

If the flame of love can't protect
the currency of heart's scars,
then it is the work of the sadness
that is always ready to jump in
when I'm unable to speak.

What can I expect from her
In the prime of her youth
when she didn't listen
to my stories as a child?

It is not good to offer
the gift of pain to anyone.
Otherwise, O God,
I would have asked You
to give my life to my enemy.

THE LAST CANDLE

Darkness prevails in my abode
and the night of sorrow
is moving back and forth.
There is only one candle left;
that too is silently squabbling
with the approaching dawn.

No news about her
and no spectacle of her beauty.
For a long time now,
there has been a perfect truce
between my eyes and ears.

The wine has made her
to throw away her veil.
Desire now has the permission
to loosen its senses as well.

I look at the necklace
of diamonds around her neck
and I wonder about the good fortune
of the diamond merchant.

The sight of wine,
Saqi's audacity,
drunken eyes.
The tavern of my imagination
is at peace with itself.

Welcome newcomers
to the land of heart's desires.
Beware, if you are simply lusting
for the joys of song and wine.

Look at me
if your eyes are looking
for an exemplar.
Listen to me
if your ears are ready
for good advice.

Because of her splendor,
Saqi is the enemy of belief
and spiritual awareness.
Her melodies steal our majesty
and mental awareness.

At the night's climax,
every corner of the place,
where the meeting had taken place,
was like the lap of the gardener
and the palm of the flower-seller.

The sheer joy
of Saqi's graceful walk
and the melodious music
coming from the harp.
A paradise for the eyes and
a heaven for the ears.

If you come to the gathering
in the morning,
you will find no joy or pain,
no cheerfulness or commotion.

Burned and devastated
from the sorrows and festivities
of the evening,
there is just one candle left.
That too is not saying a word.

I get these thoughts
from an unknown source.
though I do have a hunch.
Ghalib, I can hear the angels
write them down on a paper
with a scratching sound.

AN OATH

Come. I'm restless.
No patience.
Fed up with waiting.

Paradise to compensate
for suffering in this world?
Sorry, the intoxication offered
is not proportional to the need.

I am expelled from your assembly
for crying.
Alas! I wish I could control
my crying.

You doubt me for holding
a grudge against you.
No mist of doubt is rising
from the lovers' graves.

Use your heart
to enjoy delightful interpretations
of my poetry.
If there is no flower,
no mirror can reflect
wonders of spring.

Since you have decided to kill me,
it will be sad
if your resolve lacks
stability and strength.

Ghalib, you took an oath
to stop drinking.
Who can put trust
in your vows anymore?

THIS BUD

Throngs of sorrows
bend my head so low
that the line of eyesight
is same as that of a thread
in my lap.

I didn't get
my wounds stitched
to avoid pain.
But please understand
that this lunatic
treats pain
with utmost respect.

Ghalib, this bud
wherever it unfolds
its splendor
will bring joy
to the heart
with its resonance.

AN INSTRUMENT FILLED WITH COMPLAINTS

Enough of wandering
in the desert.
My feet are curling up
to my garb for rest.
Thorns in my sole
are like lines

that I see in the mirror
of my kneecap.

You should see
the condition of my heart
when I embrace you.
My eyes find
every strand of your hair
as something
they have known.

My whole body
is like an instrument
filled with the melodies
of complaints.
It is better for you
to not play me
in the company of others.

THE FIREPLACE

In any gathering,
when you enter
and start to speak
in your seductive style,
hearts in the paintings
stuck on the wall
start to throb.

Cypress and pine trees
will follow you like a shadow.
With your kind

of seductive height,
when you come
into the garden.

Tears are justified
under one condition.
Do they turn my liver
into a blood stream
that runs through
my eyes?

Give me the permission
to tell you
my side of the story,
O my heartless lover!
You too may get a kick
out of my tale
of suffering.

When the mirror gets a cue
from your magical eyes,
it starts talking
like a parrot.

Thorns don't speak
because their tongue
has dried up.
Wish someone
with blistered feet
will come
to the valley of thorns!

Should I not die of envy
when her frail body

is caught up
in the infinite loop
of the holy thread
around her neck?[48]

If the bud doesn't have
the passionate longing
to become a flower,
then it should better stay
in the garden and
not come to the marketplace.

You complain too much,
my poor heart.
The real happiness
of ripping up the collar
is discerned by me
when every breath
that comes out of my mouth
is coiled around a thread.

My chest is like the fireplace
that holds secrets.
It would really be dreadful
if I let those secrets slip.

Consider it to be
a mystical treasure trove
of meaning, Ghalib.
Each word that shows up
in my couplets.

---

48 Ghalib refers here to the thread that Brahmins wear around their neck.

A BRAHMIN'S PREDICTION

The full moon looks enchanting.
Her shining beauty
comparable to the sun's rays
is ravishing nevertheless.

Not allowing me to kiss,
she is watching my heart.
I know what she is thinking.
It's a good deal if it's free.

If my bowl of clay broke,
I can get another one.
It is better than the bowl of
King Jamshed.

Joy is in getting something
that you haven't asked for.
A beggar who doesn't ask
is in a better position.

When I see her,
my face radiates
with signs of well-being.
But she misunderstands
and thinks
that the patient
is feeling fine.

Let us see
what the lovers gain
from the idols.
A Brahmin has said

it's a damn good year
for them.

Farhad's axe
and the way he used it
undoubtedly made Shirin
talk to him.
Any skill one has,
always serves
a good purpose.

When a drop
merges into the river,
it becomes the river.
An action is good
if it delivers
a good outcome.

May God shower
His blessings
on the newly born
Khizr Sultan.[49]
In King's garden,
this new sapling
looks promising.

I know the actuality
of kingdom of heaven
and I won't say more.
Ghalib, it's a mythical idea
that keeps people happy.

---

[49] Written on the birth of Khizr Sultan, son of the last Mughal Emperor Bahadur Shah Zafar. He was shot and killed by the British forces during the mutiny of 1857.

Part Eight

Ghalib shows mastery over the use of imagistic language. To sustain the flow of images in quick succession, he uses different kinds of metaphors. To illustrate this point, let us look at *Heap Of Leaves In The Garden* [p. 312].

In the opening couplet, there is a touch of reification, which is an attempt to treat an abstraction (namely destination) as if it were a real thing with a mind of its own. Then the poet uses ambiguity and picks a word for destination that has multiple meanings. If wilderness is the destination, then why is it running away? And why is the speed a consideration? Will the wilderness stop running away if the speed was faster? This shows that wilderness is just a figure of speech or a cognitive metaphor for something else—maybe destiny or fate. So what the poet really means is: my effort to attain what I want in life is not yielding the result that I want. Will it make a difference if I put in more effort? Probably not.

Each step makes it clear
how far away am I
from where I need to arrive.
Watching the speed
at which I am going,
the wilderness is walking
away from me.

In the following couplet, "a thread that binds us to our eyelashes and what is behind it" is a root metaphor that talks about two worldviews or two ways of seeing the world. We look around in our state of obliviousness and then there is a deeper way of seeing the world.

We can look
at what is being talked about
and forget about it.
The real insight into things
is a thread that binds us
to our eyelashes
and what is behind it.

Picture a fire. Fire burns something down and the smoke rises and moves away in the direction of the wind. The poet describes how the fire is burning his heart and the smoke is moving away. Then there is a forced association between smoke and shadow. It is not only that the smoke is running away, it is the shadow too. When we are disassociated from our own shadow, in some ways we cease to exist. In this case, we started with a visual metaphor that the poet gradually turned into a psychological metaphor—a man without an identifiable body and a man without his self-identity.

Wild fires are burning my heart out
in the loneliness of the night.
And like the smoke around me,
my shadow is staying away from me.

When the poet passed away "the house of mirrors was desolate." The beloved stopped looking into the mirror and lost interest in her make-up. The underlying story that is not explicitly mentioned is that the beloved didn't care for the lover when he was alive but she is overwhelmed by sadness after her lover's death.

The grief of a lover passing away
should not make the beloved
to adopt a simple way of life.
The house of mirrors was desolate
when I passed away.

Blisters are small bubbles that are filled with serum and caused by friction or burning. The poet imagines himself walking on sand. The blisters, in a state of frenzy, are pearls that shine in the daylight and the zigzag path is a string in which the pearls are arranged.

Because of the blisters in my feet
the path to the wilderness
in my state of frenzy
has been illuminated
like a string of pearls.

The promise of having given up on "wanderings" enables the poet to reclaim his shadow.

Ecstasy!
Make my bed
for total relaxation.
Having given up
on my wanderings,
my bed chamber is full
like my shadow.

The lover is telling the beloved: if for the guilt of looking at you, you will behead me, then I will, like a trimmed candlewick, get another eye to look at you! "Flared flame" is the new eye that will see the beloved. Conclusion: beloved can't deny the lover the pleasure of looking at her by being cruel or a murderer.

If for the desire of just looking at you,
you would behead me,
then my power to see you will spread
like the flared flame
from a trimmed candlewick.

Imagine the state of fear when even your shadow is hiding "from the sun of Doomsday" (a mythic metaphor signifying punishment for the guilty)!

O the desperation
of the wild night of separation.
Alas! Alas!
My own shadow is hiding
from the sun of Doomsday.

Two contrasting metaphors showing differing images.

Because of you--
hundreds of wine goblets
are going around in a colorful display.
Because of me--
mirrors are showing frozen images
of my stunned eyes.

The last couplet is an example of a situational metaphor. There is a fire that is burning the heap of leaves. The first metaphor explains the cause.

Asad, fire is dripping
out of my burning eyes.
And the heap of leaves
in the garden is ablaze.

SO BE IT

I died and it satisfied no one.
If there is one more test,
please bring it on.
    So be it.

This thorny, prickly desire to see you
is still there.
But my desire could not get
a flower of solace
from the garden.
    So be it.

The lovers of wine
are drinking
straight from the decanter.
If one day Saqi is not present
in the gathering.
    So be it.

The breath of Majnun
is a source of light
for the desert,
though there is no Laila
or candle light from her black tent. [50]
    So be it.

---

[50] Majnun's breath is lighting the desert as Laila is away with her candle in her tent.

The liveliness of home
depends on the noisiness
of a celebration.
It can be a symphony of sorrows,
or the song of a wedding.
So be it.

I'm not looking for
approval or admiration.
Nor do I seek a reward.
You can say
there is no meaning
in my couplets.
So be it.

Ghalib, you're blessed
for the company
of beautiful fairies,
though you didn't live very long.
So be it.

THE WOUNDED FEATHERS

I take pleasure in walking
ahead of my executioner.
Even in the shadow,
my head is seen a couple of steps
ahead of my feet.

I was destined to be ruined
by the love of wine.

The pen wrote something bad for me
and then it could not write any further.

The sorrows of worldly affairs
robbed me of the sorrow of love.
Otherwise, the sorrow of love
was a matter of great delight for me.

In God's name,
praise the madness of my desire.
I arrive at her door before the messenger.

O interweaved tresses!
The suffering that I have gone through
will one day come before you
and demand retribution.

Hidden in my heart and liver
are wounded feathers like waves of blood.
What a misunderstanding!
I thought this was my breath.

Ghalib, those who take a vow
to attend my funeral
are the very same people
who always wished me a very long life.

A BITTER SONG

She gets upset with me
when she hears the word "complaint."
And the very mention of this
makes her mad.

I am so full of complaints
that you can easily compare me
to an instrument filled
with melodies.
Just strike me once
and then you see.

She doesn't understand
but she rectifies her actions
with a style.
Any complaint about cruelty
makes her more cruel.

In the lovers lane,
the sky filled with stars
walks like someone
who has blisters on his feet.

Why shouldn't I
be the target
of the arrow of cruelty?
If the arrow misses the target,
I go and pick it up.

It would have been better
if I had wished myself ill
from the beginning.
I long for some good to happen
but only bad happens.

My cries
used to reach the sky
but now they come
to my lips
and go nowhere.

My pen is like
that of Barbud[51]
in the gathering of poets.
And like him,
it starts to sing
praises of the king.

O Emperor,
stars are your soldiers,
and the sun is your flag.
How can we repay
the good that you have done?

Even if we collect
the wealth of seven continents,
it will just be a ransom money
for your forces.

When the moon
turns into a crescent,
this monthly ritual
is nothing more than the moon
rubbing its head
at your threshold.

I am being disrespectful
of etiquettes
for writing a ghazal.
But this is the result
of your kindness
in creating
a new style of writing.

---

51 Barbud was a singer in King Khusrao's court and sang his praises.

Ghalib, I seek your forgiveness
for singing a bitter song today.
There is more pain
in my heart
than is normally the case.

IF IT DIDN'T DRIP FROM MY EYES

You challenge every word that I say,
telling me: who are you?
You tell me: what kind of conversation
is this one?

Neither the flame has this miracle,
nor the lightening has this style.
Will someone tell me what that temptress
is really like?

I am envious
that he is speaking with you.
Otherwise, I'm not concerned
that the enemy will mislead you.

My blood is working as a glue
making my dress stick to my body.
My collar doesn't need any stitch
or patch at this time.

My heart must have burned
with my body.
What are you trying to gain
by sifting through my ashes?

I'm not convinced
by something racing up and down
in my veins.
If it didn't drip from my eyes,
then it is not blood.

What is one thing that is precious
and dear to me about paradise?
Nothing except the pink,
musk-scented wine.

I will drink wine if I can see
two or four decanters full of wine.
What are the glasses, bowls, goblets,
and tumblers?

Now I have lost my power to speak
but even if it were there,
with what confidence could I say:
"This is what I really want."

Because Ghalib has become King's courtier,
he is just trying to show off.
Otherwise, what is his standing
in this town?

I NEEDED SEVERAL HEARTS

I poked fun at her
and she didn't say a thing.
She would have given me a mouthful
if she had been drinking like me.

Either you are a calamity or a spirit.
It doesn't matter.
I wish you were made for me.

If my life was filled
with so much suffering,
then dear God,
you should have given me
several hearts as well.

Ghalib,
she would have seen some merit
in my yearning,
if I had lived a little longer.
Alas!

DRINKING NEAR ZAMZAM WELL

Strange people in your party
are kissing the wine glasses.
And I remain waiting for your invitation,
while playing with my dried lips.

How can I complain
about my absolute ruination.
I know how the blue painted sky
is playing tricks with me.

I will write letters to you
without any rhyme or reason.
It's not the subject matter;
it's just your name I'm in love with,
and nothing else.

Last night, we were drinking
near the Zamzam well.[52]
In the morning, we washed the stains
from our pilgrim's garbs.

My heart was trapped by my eyes.
But looking closely these are the rings
of your snare.

There is news:
The King will take his bath
following his recovery from illness.
Let us see how fortunate
this bath proves to be.[53]

Ghalib, this constant yearning
for the beloved
has made me a loser.
Otherwise, I had merit
in the kind of person I were.

• •

52 A well near Kaaba, the sacred place of pilgrimage.

53 This couplet was written around 1853 when Emperor Bahadur Shah Zafar recovered from a prolonged illness.

SPRING

The spring came with such splendor
that even sun and moon
turned spectators.

O the residents of this earth,
look what the spring has brought.
This is called beautifying the world.

The earth has changed
from one bend to a curve.
It is putting to shame
the face of the blue colored sky.

When the grass couldn't find
a place to grow,
it became algae
on the water's surface.

So that it can look at the greenery
and the flowers,
narcissus[54] has received eyes to see.

The air smells of wine.
Breathing is no different
from drinking.

Why would the people
not rejoice Ghalib?
Our God-fearing King
has recovered from illness.

---

54 Narcissus – eye shaped flower.

THE EMPTY TAVERNS

I am a friend, but oblivious.
My mind thinks high,
but I'm extremely humble.
If you move away from me,
my seat will be empty too.

The world is filled with people,
but where are the courageous ones?
Goblets and decanters are filled with wine,
but why do taverns look empty?

MY STORY

She is not interested
in listening to my story.
And that too coming from
my own mouth.

Don't ask me
about her killing glances.
See the blood dripping
from my eyes.

What would my friends say
at my funeral,
other than to talk about the madness
of my spoken words?

I'm loitering in the desert
of my own thoughts.
Getting lost is my trademark.

Standing face to face,
my rival blinked when he saw
the command I have
over the spoken word.

My worth is no more
than the stone on the pathway.
My expensive being
is now going rather cheap.

I'm like the whirlwind
in the path of restlessness.
I'm a creation
of a dust storm of desire.

I couldn't locate her mouth
thereby exposing
my ignorance.

Ghalib, my withering body
has humbled me.
My old age arrived
at the peak of my youth.

THE FEVER OF LOVE

That frisky idol
in the arms of my rival
is a pretty ugly sight.
Imagine painter Mani[55]
doing his masterpiece
with peocock's feet
instead of a brush.

I question your manners
while you listen playfully
to my amazing story.
A tale of sadness
requires a bit of insanity
to be told.

The fever of love
is like the heat
of the candle's flame.
It demands passage
through the veins
to reach the liver.

BUDS UNFOLDING TO EMBRACE YOU

The garden
is so much in love
with you.
When buds unfold

[55] Mani – a citizen of Babylon and a famous painter.

to become flowers
they hold you
in their arms.

The wall
of your forgetfulness
is growing taller
with each passing moment.
But my laments
are not accepting defeat.
They are ready
to reach higher
and higher.

Sorrow teaches you
the art of taking things
in a stride.
The scar you see
is the result
of your eye
of disapproval.

A CONFRONTATIONAL IDOL

A wound that has any chance
of healing, O God,
give it to my enemy.

A look at her tiny,
henna-colored fingers
makes me think
of my own heart.

I can see
a tiny drop of blood.

Why are you concerned
with the lack of ambition
of your lovers?
In this place, no one listens
to what goes on
in the lives of others.

The dagger has not shown
its face to the liver.
The knife has not asked about
the well-being of the throat.

Pity a hundred times!
Ghalib's pleas
have remained
unsuccessful
for having
a confrontational idol.

FAREWELL NIGHTINGALE!

A coating of mercury
makes the glass
to become a mirror.
The commotion
of my impatient heart
defines who I am.

The flowers have opened
their bosoms
to say farewell.
Nightingale, move on
because the days
of the spring are over.

WHEN A UNION IS REALLY A UNION

If one is required to maintain dignity
and control movement,
then union is no better than separation.
What we need is a lively sweetheart
and a lover driven by the madness of love.

I will surely get a kiss from those lips.
Yes! What I need is the euphoric spirit
and the courage of a drunkard.

NEED A ROWDY FRIEND

We should adore the good ones
as much as we can.
And if they want you,
what more you could ask for.

It is good to be cautious
about our contacts with
habitual drunkards.

Better to keep oneself away
from their company in the tavern.

What did the heart think
before it fell in love with you?
It surely deserves spanking.

Don't be in too much of a rush
to tear your collar.
When the spring comes,
you will get a signal.

Friendship
is the veil of indifference.
Stop hiding
your face from me.

My rival's attempt to harm me
made him a loser.
How strong is the enemy
we have to see.

What do we need
if we wish to disgrace ourselves?
A rowdy friend will do.

Think of the one who has put
all his hopes on dying.
His disappointment is worth noticing.

Ignorant --
These moon-faced beauties
deserve good-looking lovers

Asad,
you pine for the beautiful ones.
Have you looked at your own face?

HEAP OF LEAVES IN THE GARDEN

Each step makes it clear
how far away am I
from where I need to arrive.
Watching the speed
at which I am going,
the wilderness is walking
away from me.

We can look
at what is being talked about
and forget about it.
The real insight into things
is a thread that binds us
to our eyelashes
and what is behind it.

Wild fires are burning my heart out
in the loneliness of the night.
And like the smoke around me,
my shadow is staying away from me.

The grief of a lover passing away
should not make the beloved
to adopt a simple way of life.
The house of mirrors was desolate
when I passed away.

Because of the blisters in my feet
the path to the wilderness
in my state of frenzy
has been illuminated
like a string of pearls.

Ecstasy!
Make my bed
for total relaxation.
Having given up
on my wanderings,
my bed chamber is full
like my shadow.

If for the desire
of just looking at you,
you would behead me,
then my power
to see you will fan out
like the flared flame
from a trimmed candlewick.

O the desperation
of the wild night of separation.
Alas! Alas!
My own shadow is hiding
from the sun of Doomsday.

Because of you--
hundreds of wine goblets
are going around
in a colorful display.
Because of me--
mirrors are showing

frozen images
of my stunned eyes.

Asad, fire is dripping
out of my burning eyes.
And the heap of leaves
in the garden is ablaze.

A STRANGER WITH YOUR LETTER

With her critical disposition
I find it hard to make her listen
to the woes of my heart.
It's not a good conversation
when she won't let me say
what I want to say.

I'm calling her,
but my craving heart,
something strange can happen.
And then she may not resist
coming to me.

Treating it like a game,
she can leave me.
Or forget me.
I wish it happens this way,
but without the pain
of gamesmanship.

A stranger is moving around
with your letter in hand.

So obvious for me to see.
And if someone were to ask
there was no way for him to hide it.

Your tenderness be damned
I'm not questioning your goodness.
My issue is different.
If I had you standing by my side,
how will I stop myself
from touching you?

Who can say whose glorious
manifestation is this?
The Creator has dropped the veil.
Who can lift it now?

I'm not waiting for death to come.
She will come whether I like it or not.
Your coming is different.
I can't even call you,
if you don't come.

The burden that has fallen on me,
I can't live with.
A situation that has arisen
I can't deal with.

You can't do anything
about passionate love.
This is like a fire Ghalib.
You can neither start it,
nor end it.

THE GOBLET'S EYELASHES

If in my fit of madness
I rip up my collar and expose myself.
The wound of my heart,
like a day break, will become my collar.

Such is the splendor of your beauty
that even if I think of you,
my eyes turn my heart
into a place of wonder.

My heart is waiting to be shattered.
God knows for how long!
Should a piece of glass complain
about the stinginess of the mountain? [56]

If her intoxicating eyes
can defeat the tavern,
the hairline crack in the goblet
will become eyelashes
lowering its sight in shame.

To the tresses of the beloved,
here is my written commitment of love.
Your sideburns are fully acceptable
though they might cause
some inconvenience.[57]

---

[56] The beloved is stonehearted like a mountain while the heart is like a piece of glass.

[57] Presumably, written for a male lover.

TEARS AS SHARP AS A SWORD

I want her to visit me in my dream
and give me some consolation,
if my throbbing heart would let me
get some sleep first.

It kills me to see you crying
when I make fun of you.
No one can show tears
which are as sharp as a sword
as you do.

You can kill me by just showing me
the quiver of your lips.
If you don't want to kiss me,
at least say something nice.

O Saqi, your hatred aside,
let me drink through my cupped hands.
If you can't give me a cup
that's okay as long as I get some wine.

Asad, my hands and feet
swelled with joy, when she said,
"Will you massage my feet for a little while?"

ON THE BED

The palpitation of my heart
is intertwined with every thread of my bed.
My head is troubling the pillow
and the body a burden on the bed.

When tears fall from my eyes,
they are lost in the wilderness of my lap.
My heart is miserably lethargic
and is just resting on the bed.

My sickness has brought the good news
that you came to see me.
The candle by the bed-rest flared up and
my luck brightened as I lay on the bed.

Intense restlessness is fueling a twister
in this night of separation.
The morning sun of the Doomsday
is shaking up threads on the bed.

I can get the smell of her tresses
while I rest my head on my pillow.
My imagination is richer than
Zulekha[58] dreaming of her lover.

Ghalib, what can I say
about the condition of my heart
during this time of separation.
Each thread is a thorn on the bed.

---

58 Zulekha dreaming of her lover Joseph.

THIS SEASON'S POTENTIAL

I'm afraid that our romantic relationship
might lead to "go for the jugular"
kind of situation.
Pride in friendship is destructive.
You might turn into an enemy.

Ghalib, this season's growth potential
will be in jeapardy if flowers do not get
as tall as cypresses.

EXISTENCE AND NONEXISTENCE

Prayers for redressing grievances
are not meant to have notes of a melody.
Lamentations do not depend on flute
as an accompaniment to be effective.

Why do gardeners plant bitter pumpkins
when the garden is not looking for a bowl
to drink wine?

You are manifest in everything
we see in the universe,
but there is nothing anywhere
that is exactly like You.

Don't be deceived by the illusions of reality.
Let everyone say that unreal is real,
but it is not.

If we let go of happiness,
we shall not be saddened.
If there is no spring,
there will be no autumn.

Why do pious non-drinkers
reject the wine?
It is not something
that honeybees regurgitate.[59]

Ghalib, let us not talk about
existence and nonexistence
because these are concepts
and they are not real.
But then, who are you?
O, "I'm not."

THE DUST OF DIAMONDS

Don't ask me about the ingredients
of this ointment that I apply to heal
the wounds of my heart.
Let me say --
the dust of diamonds
that pierces the heart further
is the main one.

59 Pious Muslims who do not drink wine like to consume honey. The poet is mocking them by saying: What is so good about the "honeybee's vomit" that you hate wine?

Your long-lasting obliviousness
has finally produced
a glance that looks at me
but it is less than a full glance.

WHEN YOU BAD MOUTH GHALIB

Jealousy or envy
has no place near me.
I would rather die
than long for her.

Behind her veil I think she is making
a connection with my rival.
Her veil is just a façade;
it is not the real thing.

My rivals listen to you and think:
When you bad-mouth Ghalib,
you are not doing a good thing.

A TIME TO SEE ASAD

When you drink wine,
your lips change its color.
The curved upper surface of the cup
turns into the eyes of a flower-picker.

When will my frenzied heart
get to hear some encouraging words.
For a long time,
it has been looking
just for the comfort of a pillow.

No wonder,
they do not hear
the cries of the nightingale.
Dew is acting like a cotton
in the flowers' ears.

Asad is dying!
For God's sake,
it is time for the one
who was unfaithful to him
to see him.
Put aside your shyness
and get rid of your pride.

Part Nine

French philosopher Paul Ricoeur (1913-2005) defined metaphor as a living entity that opened a new window to understanding the meaning of life or natural phenomena. He was of the view that metaphors enabled us to look at the world in new ways and thus become aware of our own creative capacities. Ghalib uses his typical imagistic language in *Pearls of Defeat* [p. 344] but with a difference. Each metaphor is like a truism (something obvious or self-evident) that has the potential to teach us something new.

The opening couplet of this ghazal addresses a larger question: How do we communicate with our ailing body? And there is a more specific question: How should I communicate with my body's wounds? Behind the visual metaphor ("wound has a mouth to speak"), there is a non-linguistic metaphor that says that unless we become quiet, we can't listen to our body.

Unless the wound
has a mouth to speak,
it is difficult
to communicate with it.

The following couplet makes a reference to the familiar Laila-Majnun love story. Two strong metaphors are thrown in: the world as a "dust storm" and hair hanging in a "corkscrew curl." There is a tension here between the subjective reality (the lover's fascination for the beloved's hair) and the objective reality (man's role in a turbulent world controlled by a distant and indifferent God).

The world appears to be a dust storm
raised by Majnun's frenzy.
How long can we go on thinking
about Laila's lock of hair
hanging in a corkscrew curl?

Pessimism leads to more pessimism. Sadness begets more sadness. What would calm a heart that is already hurting? More pain.

Sadness will not transform itself
into happiness
even if the beloved
gives her amorous attention.
Yes, but someone can become pain
and enter the heart.

Sadness doesn't transform into happiness in a moment. It takes time to undo "knots of the heart." Perhaps, more crying is the remedy in this case.

Don't stop me from crying, my friend.
One needs time to undo
knots of the heart.

Some situations have no easy solution. If extreme solutions don't work, an ordinary move is unlikely to succeed.

When piercing of my liver
didn't get her attention,
then what could tearing up
of my collar might achieve?

There is only so much you can do to sustain a difficult outcome.

I find pieces of my liver
have entered the veins
of thorns and flowers.
How long should I be held responsible
for flowering of the desert?

Human eye is incapable of seeing through the lightening. If God is the lightening then it is impossible to see Him or know Him. He can be known, if at all, through inner seeing.

The failure of my eyesight
proves that You are the lightening
that burns the spectacle.
You are not the one
whose spectacle
could be seen by anyone.

Every rejection and failure in life is like a "pearl" because it paves the way for new learning and greater success.

Every rock and brick thrown at you
is a pearl of defeat.
There is no loss if someone wishes
to trade with madness.

When do you give up longing for something that is out of your reach? This is an example of a dead or missing metaphor, which is about a decision in your life—when do you stop a particular pursuit?

The whole life was not sufficient
for your promises
to come to fruition.

Who has the time
to continue to long for you?

The following couplet presents the profile of a creative person. Modern research on creative types has demonstrated that they are the "crazy ones" driven by a passion unknown to ordinary folks.

The personality of a creative person
is inherently wild and pessimistic.
This is not the agony that one could fake.

The danger of overreaction to defeat can't be minimized. The metaphor of a "broken hand" highlights the risk of a self-inflicted injury that could make one more vulnerable to failure.

In the idleness of frenzy
you play the game
of striking your head.
But if your hands are broken,
what could you possibly do?

Great advice to an aspiring young poet: don't rush to learn the techniques of writing. First, work on your heart. Make it less rigid and more open. Let it flow. And then you will write great poetry!

Asad, the poetry that captures the beauty
of the brightness of candle
will come with the passage of time.
First, you have to produce
a free-flowing heart.

A REALLY SHARP DAGGER

Why wouldn't she
 keep her eyes away from me?
A sick man has been advised
rest and recuperation.
That's why.

While I'm dying
I carry with me
my desire to see her.
But to my bad luck,
her dagger is really sharp.

Asad, looking at the cheeks
of the flowers
reminded me of her face.
The explosive onset of spring
is leading to all kind of
exciting thoughts.

WHAT CAN I SAY?

If he has fallen in love with her,
he is just being human.
If he becomes my rival, so be it.
After all, he is a messenger.
    What can I say?

I insist that she shouldn't come today
but I can't stop her from coming.
I have so many complaints against death.
    What can I say?

He routinely lingers on
around her alley.
It's an enemy territory now.
    What can I say?

She has some miraculous power
through which she continues
to deceive me.
Without my saying a word,
she knows what's in my mind.
    What can I say?

She asks for my well-being
when we meet in the bazar.
Standing by the roadside, really?
    What can I say?

You don't seem to care
from where the thread
of my faithfulness starts.
I have something in my hand.
What is it?
    What can I say?

She thinks
the questions that I ask are crazy.
I can't fight with that.
I'm indifferent to answers.
    What can I say?

If you write good poetry,
jealousy is the result.
What can you do?
Oppression is the price
of literary talent.
    What can I say?

Ghalib, no one has said
that you are bad
except that you have lost your mind.
    What can I say?

THE WHETSTONE

Looking at my attempt
to shed my garments,
my nudity tied me down
to my body
that I could not shed.

Her sharp glances
that I keep hidden like a miser
have turned me into a whetstone.
This way she enhances
the sharpness of her glances
and I keep my connection with her.

She is content that
she doesn't care about me.
But she knows it well
that she is in my thoughts
secretly.

When the value
of my house of sorrow
was being assessed,
I was told
that I was the sole cause
of its desolation.

My beloved, the kafir,
becomes suspicious.
I wish that was not the case.
Such is my desire to listen
to the songs of the nightingale.

The tumult of the Doomsday
didn't let me rest in peace.
I went to my grave
carrying my desire
for a restful time.

You must fulfill
your promise to come.
What is this style?
Why have you given me
the responsibility of guarding
my own house?

Yes, the arrival of spring
is a joyful time.
Cheers! Cheers!
I am once again possessed
by my madness
to write ghazals.

God has blessed my brother
with a new life.
Ghalib, Mirza Yusuf [60] is my Joseph.

THE MAGIC OF POETRY

Even in my days of happiness
I have repeated God's name.
Hidden under my lips
is the rosary of the faithful.

Thanks to my poetry,
the doors to my suffering heart opened.
It was sheer magic that my words
opened this combination lock.

O God!
Who should I approach
to get appreciation
for my madness?
Now I am envious
how comfortable
is the life for the prisoners.

It is in my nature to find joy in grief.
What should I do?
My desire drives me to seek longings
that have failed to come to fruition.

60 Mirza Yusuf was Ghalib's brother who suffered from mental illness. He died in 1857.

Ghalib, after you fell in love
you became like me.
You used to advise me
against falling in love Mirza Sahib.[61]

THE TEST

In the presence of His Majesty,
poets were putting to test their poetical skills.
In the garden, flower-loving singers
were gathered to test their lyrical chords.

Majnun and Farhad were obsessed
with the beauty, grandeur, and
tresses of their beloveds.
My challenge is different.
I'm worried whether I will be hanged

We shall examine later how bold
was the resolve of the mountain-digger.
We have to see whether the man
had the strength to take the bad news
in its stride.[62]

The breeze from Egypt shall not bring
comfort to the old man from Canaan.

61 Mirza is the title used by those who claim Turkish descent. Sahib during those days was respectful speech for a British officer. The combination is a satirical tone that the poet wishes to convey.

62 The bad news that Shirin had died.

It was merely testing Joseph's fragrance
from his clothes.[63]

She has joined the gathering.
Look, don't complain later
that you were unaware.
It's a test of the patience of
those present.

Your arrow should better stay in my heart.
But I don't mind if it goes through my liver.
My beautiful loving idol, it's not me;
but it's you who are being tested.

The infinite loop of the rosary
can't impress anyone; it's just a show.
The real test of a Shaikh and a Brahmin
is how true are they to their faith.

Stay where you are, my patient heart.
There is nothing to be gained
by being impatient.
It is a test of the curled tresses, once again.

I'm just waiting for the poison of sorrow
to creep into my veins and nerves.
The real test occurs when it reaches
my my mouth and throat.

Will she come and visit my home?
There is no promise yet.
Let us see Ghalib.
Not only she but the whole sky is testing me.

---

63 Reference to a Koranic story about Jacob and his son Joseph.

MY LOVE STORY

Even when she thinks of doing something nice,
she is suddenly overcome with shame,
remembering her betrayals.

O God, the longing of my heart is having
an opposite affect.
The more I try to bring her toward me,
the more she moves away from me.

She has a bad disposition and
my love story is rather long.
Although I try to be brief,
even the messenger is drained by me.

Over there, she is mistrustful of me.
Over here, I'm physically exhausted.
She is not asking anything and
I can hardly speak.

Let me catch my breath.
O the feeling of hopelessness!
The edge of my beloved's thought
is slipping away from me.

Protocol aside,
I am keenly watching her.
But I can't bear the pain
when others too watch her.

The woes of my love life
have already wounded my feet.

I can neither run,
nor stand still on my two feet.

What a calamity Ghalib
that your rival has become
her travel companion --
that kafir I couldn't leave
even in God's care.

WHEN EVEN THE MIRROR IS NOT ON YOUR SIDE

Our sanity can be questioned,
if we just look around.
We find how impermanent the world is,
if we see deeply.
Otherwise, it is just fluttering
of the eyelashes.

I do not know
how you will erase the scars
coming from voices
that you broke promises.
When even the mirror
is not on your side,
there is a problem.

We should not break our connection
with our well-being
as we go through twists and turns of life.
Showing an outlook of humility
is the best protection.

When fidelity comes before love,
it is meaningless.
True lovers are naturally crazy
when the spring comes.

TRAPPED IN HER TRESSES

I am so frail in my present condition
that if you invite me to your gathering,
I can assure you that no one
will even notice me.

I would not be surprised
if looking at my condition
she might be overwhelmed
by kindness and compassion.
Only if someone could take me
to her presence!

If you don't want to show me your face,
that's fine with me.
But to show your displeasure,
could you just lift the veil and
show me your eyes?

She is so thrilled with my arrest
that if I were her tangled tresses,
she would keep me trapped
using her comb.

A KID'S PLAYGROUND

The world is a kid's playground
in front of me.
Many acts are played out
in front of my eyes.
Each day when the sun rises and
each night when it sets.

The throne of Solomon
is a source of amusement for me.
I have heard the talk
about Jesus raising the dead.

If the universe is just a name,
it is not acceptable to me.
There is an illusion that things
do exist, but it is not a reality
for me.

My going into the desert raises
such dust that it conceals
its very existence.
But the river is humble.
It rubs its forehead in the mud,
when it sees the flow of my tears.

Don't ask me what happens to me
in your absence.
Just see what happens
to your complexion
when you just look at me.

You are right when you say
that I have become
self-centered and egoistic.
Why shouldn't I be?
I'm sitting in front of an idol
who looks just like a mirror.

Watch me deliver
a flamboyant speech,
if someone just take the trouble
of putting a goblet of wine
in front of me.

It gives a semblance of hate
and I should give up my envy.
How can I tell others
not to say her name
in my presence?

My faith pulls me toward it
though disbelief
is also pulling me
in another direction.
My idol, she attracts me!
Mosque is behind me
and I see a Temple in front of me.

I am a lover but playing tricks
with my beloved is my passion.
My credentials as a lover
are so impressive
that even Laila tells Majnun
"you're not good enough"
in front of me.

Union gives happiness
but we shouldn't die like this.
The longing for the night of separation
suddenly appeared before me.

An ocean of blood
is rising like the high tide.
Maybe this is it.
Let us see what comes
in front of my eyes now.

Though my hands
have lost some grip,
my eyes still show some spark.
Just leave the decanter
and the goblet in front of me.

He is in the same line of work,
he is my drinking buddy,
and he is my confidante.
Why do you say bad things about Ghalib?
Well, that too in front of me.

WHAT THE THE BOAT CAPTAIN DID TO US

If I describe my condition,
you tell me, "What's the purpose?"
If you speak to me like this,
what can I say?

Please do not say it even in sarcasm,
"Am I a tyrant?"

It is my habit to agree with you
whatever you say.

They may be lancets
but they cut deep into my heart
and they become part of me.
So why I shouldn't call those
flirty glances friendly?

Small arrow makes a small wound.
So it's not a source of great comfort.
It's only the sword that makes the heart
to open up.

The one who is complaining,
don't be his supporter.
If someone is really nasty,
you don't have to copy him.

Sometime we self-diagnose
and identify a soul-crushing malady.
At other times,
it is only about the medicine
that didn't work.

Sometime we complain about
sorrow overtaking us.
At other times, we talk about
patience that is ready to flee.

When life is cut short,
give the blood money to the killer.
When the tongue is slashed,
bless the dagger.

If she doesn't love me anymore,
it doesn't matter
because she is still my beloved.
Her free flowing walk
and her flirtatious behavior
is just enough for me.

If the spring is in a hurry to leave,
so be it.
Let us talk about the freshness
of the garden and
the freshness of the breeze.

Ghalib, when the boat has reached the shore,
why complain to God
about what the boat captain did to us
during the trip?

ON RAISING ASAD'S DEAD BODY

Crying in love made me bolder.
I have been so completely cleansed
that I have become pious.

When I couldn't pay for the wine,
I had to barter my goblet and decanter.
Now, I have neither any money
to pay for the wine,
nor anything to drink wine with.
So two accounts were settled
at one time.

Your vagabondage
earned you some notoriety.
But moving around
made you smarter too.

Who says that the cry of the nightingale
has no influence?
In rose's veil a hundred thousand livers
have been sliced open.

Don't ask me about the existence
and nonexistence of those who love.
They were like leaves and straw
who burned in their own fire.

I complained to her
about her indifference.
But with her one glance
I was reduced to dust.

Yesterday --
she raised Asad's dead body
with such lack of respect
that seeing this
even his enemies were filled
with extreme sorrow.

WHEN DECANTER BECAME THE CYPRESS TREE

There is such intoxication in the air
that even the musical instruments
are drunk.

The decanter has become the cypress tree
standing by the melodious river.

Oh my friends, please do not stop me
from disrupting's my beloved's celebration.
In that gathering,
my laments are the most trusted songs.

AN ENDLESS OCEAN OF TEARS

The amorous playfulness of teeth
is for good laughter.
The claim of friendship
is a step toward
bringing happiness in life.

Before it is born,
the bud is reflecting
on the fate of the flower to be.
With its head in its knees,
it is imagining the laughter to follow.

In the pain of sadness,
the luxury of restlessness
is not allowed.
Otherwise, the laughter will follow
after we have dug our teeth
into our heart.

My friends do not see
the fire hidden inside.
My heart is a nonstop sea of tears,
though her lips search for laughter.

A SPECTACLE

The careless beauty
is a buyer of goods
needed for a spectacle.
With mirror on her knees,
she is finding
new ways to present herself.

O my power of self-consciousness,
how long will you keep losing yourself
in the colorful displays?
When the open eyes are shut,
the show is lost.

PEARLS OF DEFEAT

Unless the wound
has a mouth to speak,
it is difficult
to communicate with it.

The world appears to be a duststorm
raised by Majnun's frenzy.
How long can we go on thinking
about Laila's lock of hair
hanging in a corkcrew curl?

Sadness will not transform itself
into happiness
even if the beloved
gives her amorous attention.

Yes, but someone can become pain
and enter the heart.

Don't stop me from crying, my friend.
One needs time to undo
the knots of the heart.

When piercing of my liver
didn't get her attention,
then what could tearing up
of my collar might achieve?

I find pieces of my liver
have entered the veins
of thorns and flowers.
For how long
should I be held responsible
for flowering of the desert?

The failure of my eyesight
proves that You are the lightening
that burns the spectacle.
You are not the one
whose spectacle
could be seen by anyone.

Every rock and brick thrown at you
is a pearl of defeat.
There is no loss if someone wishes
to trade with madness.

My whole life was not sufficient
for your promises to come to fruition.
Who has the time
to continue to long for you?

The personality of a creative person
is inherently wild and pessimistic.
This is not the agony that one could fake.

In the idleness of frenzy
you play the game
of striking your head.
But if your hands are broken,
what could you possibly do?

Asad, the poetry that captures the beauty
of the brightness of candle
will come with the passage of time.
First, you have to produce
a free-flowing heart.

SOME DO'S AND DON'TS

Jesus may have raised the dead,
but my suffering is different.
Who can subside my pain?
Who will perform this miracle?

Although there are religious laws,
what can one do
about the murderer
who doesn't use
any conventional weapons?

Her walk is like an arrow
shot from a fully strung bow.

How can I enter a heart
like that?

She rudely interrupts anyone
who speaks.
It is better to just listen to her.

My speech is incoherent
in a fit of mayhem.
In God's name,
no one should try to make
any sense of my babbling

If someone talks ill of you,
it is better not to listen.
Don't say anything
if you're wronged.

Try to stop if someone follows
the wrong path.
Forgive, if someone makes a mistake.

Is there anyone
who is not in need of help and care?
What can we do?
There is only so much we can do.

What did Khizr
do to Alexander?[64]
Where can we find

64 Khizr was supposed to be Alexander's guide during the latter's journey to the Fountain of Eternity but he abandoned him for a selfish reason: to gain eternal life for himself.

a dependable guide?

Ghalib, when all hope is lost,
what is the use of complaining
about anyone?

GHALIB'S PEN

There is lot of sorrow in the world,
but there is no shortage of wine.
I am like a slave of Saqi
who lives in the paradise.
Do I need to worry about anything?

I know about your style and
manners, and if you are delighted
by my rival's company,
where is the tyranny in it?

Ghalib's pen scatters fire all around.
I too believe in it.
But is there any spark left
in his writing?

RAISING THE DEAD

I go to my garden
for some peace of mind
but it frightens me as weak of heart.
The shadows of the flowering trees

appear like black snakes
reminiscent of her black tresses.

There is a belief that the edge of the sword
is like the banks of a stream.
If that's true then I'm like the greenery
that grows in the poisonous waters.

I'm intensely watching the break up
of my heart.
Someone is pushing me
to the house of mirrors.

Lament is the center of this world
and the world itself
is nothing more than a fistful of dust.
The sky is like an egg of the ringdove.

When I was alive, she would ask me
to rise and leave her company.
Now let us see --
how will she "raise" me since I'm dead.

WHY?

The pathway has been trampled
by the royal horses.
Why would the dust not brag
about its good luck?

When the king himself comes
to see the garden of tulips,

why would the people
not like the garden of tulips?

I'm not dying to have a stroll
in the garden.
But why would I not consume
breeze of the spring season?

THOUSAND DESIRES

There are thousand desires.
Each one is worth dying for.
Many of my wishes
were satisfied, but many remain
unfulfilled.

Why should my slayer be afraid?
This killing is not on her neck.
My blood has been flowing
through my wet eyes all my life.

We've heard a lot about
Adam's expulsion from the paradise.
But there was a greater disgrace
in how I was expelled from your alley.

The myth about your height
will be shattered, O Cruel One,
if you let your curls to unfurl.

I want her to receive letters
written only by me and no one else.
With this hope
I leave my home each morning
with my pen stuck behind my ear.

For long,
wine drinking has been associated
with my name.
It's time that the world
should see once again
the goblet of Jamshed.

Those who would have appreciated
my wounds,
they turned out to be
more wounded
by the sword of tyranny.

When you're in love,
there is no difference
between living and dying.
We live by seeing the idol
who kills us by her beauty.

For God's sake,
don't lift the veil over Kaaba.
Who knows the idol is found
there too.[65]

[65] Historically, Kaaba is located near places where idols were worshipped during pre-Islamic time.

Ghalib, what was preacher doing
near the door to the tavern?
But I know one thing for sure.
Yesterday, I saw him going in
while I was on my way out.

AN EGG IN A CAGE

If I'm too much of a burden
for the mountain
I'm ready to become its echo.
Speak honestly, O Flaming Spark,
what should I really be?

An egg in a cage
is free of hair and feathers.
It is the potential for new life,
if it could free itself
from the cage.

THE DESERT OF MY EYE

The pleasure of drinking
is spoiled because of Saqi's indifference.
The slow movement of the decanter
is making me doze off.

Except for the wound
that your sword
of seductiveness gave me,

I have no desire in my heart.
The collar of my imagination
was ripped by you.

Asad, I can't see anything
in the frenzy of my desire.
The desert of my eye
is just a fistful of dust.

JESUS'S LIPS

Jesus's lips
are rocking
the cradle.
Such is the deep slumber
of the victims
of her lips.

THE WAVE OF WINE

Water signals the flood's arrival.
The footprints on the narrow pathway
give the appearance of fingers in the ear.
Those footprints shall be wiped out.

Whose intoxicating eyes have turned
the gathering of wine drinkers
into a house of frenzy?
It seems that the wave of wine is hiding
like the pulse of a fairy in the decanter.

THE OUTCOME OF MY YEARNING

I'm waiting to see
the outcome of my yearning.
My desire may come to fruition
but it is unpredictable.
I should better act as a spectator.

WHEN THE INK IS SPILLED

Imagine what happens
when the ink is spilled on paper
at the time of writing!
This is the picture of my condition
during the night of separation.

STRAWS OF REED

With the crowding of my laments,
I'm unable to express my desire.
In my silence, I hold hundreds
of straws of reed in my teeth
to express my humility.

Formality aside, the kindness
of my mercurial beloved is deadlier.
Her intimate glance of seductiveness
is fatal like a sharp sword.

Too much grief
has destroyed my happiness.
The morning of Eid appears to be
like the days
when I used to tear up my collar.

Bring your heart and your faith
as the currency if you want to
bargain with Saqi.
In this bazar everything sells,
including the goblet.

Lovers are raised by grief
in the arms of calamities.
Their lamps remain lit
like the coral in the sea
of a sandstorm.

A WOUND THAT GETS WORST

Your seductive charm silently starts a spectacle.
Coming straight from your heart,
your glances are laced with antimony.

When the breeze enters the layers of the bud,
it finds no opening and sweats in frustration.
It has no choice other than to shine
as morning dew on the petals of the bud.

To ask the lover's chest how it received
the sharp glance of the beloved is really futile.
The wound was deep infesting the air around it.

HEART VERSUS EYES

When the beloved's tresses
are arranged by the breeze
and its fragrance reaches the deer
in the Tattar desert,
they start to produce
the perfumed musk.

Whose glorious manifestation
are we searching? O God!
In all six directions,
the universe has turned itself
into a mirror.

The tightness of space around me
reduces to dust the wildness of my desire.
If I continue to be constrained
in this manner, then the vastness of desert
will be nothing more than a snare.

The heart is suing the eyes for damages.
The case is now before the court
for a face to face trial.

The dew is like a splash of water
on the mirror of the rose petals.
It is time, O Nightingale, to say goodbye
to the spring.

I need to do something quick
about the promise of my beloved.
Whether she comes or not
I shall go on waiting here.
Yes, on the same spot.

Do not go into the vale of Majnun
without a veil covering your face.
Behind each particle,
beats a tumultuous heart.

O Nightingale,
collect a fistful of straw
to make your nest.
The storm foretells
coming of the spring.

Don't lose your heart.
If there is nothing new,
then it will be a nice walk.
O my haughty beloved,
the mirror has many images.

Ignorance makes us believe
that we shall live forever.
Asad lives in happiness
and is not afraid of death.
It can come anytime.
What is it waiting for?

AN UNCONTROLLED OCEAN OF DESIRE

Maybe I should give you a mirror
so that you can watch your own spectacle.
Where can I find another
whom people will consider as magnificent?

My yearning for you has brought me
to the assembly of your thoughts,
though I'm unable to see you.
The black spot of my eye has become
the black spot of my love.

Who has spoken into the ear of love?
Tell me, O God!
The magic of waiting for the beloved
is another name for the fulfillment of desire.

There is a crowd of hopelessness
suppressing me.
What can I do with a handful of dust?
Would you call it a desert?

Hidden behind the longing of my eyes
bedewed with tears, there is an uncontrolled
ocean of desire.

It is required for the flower of desire to bloom.
On a morning of a spring day, we can call it
the cotton wool of the decanter.

Ghalib, please don't pay attention
to the preacher when he calls you
"not up to scratch."
Is there anyone
who is universally praised?

BUT THERE IS GOD

The dew on the tulips is there for a reason.
The scars of my heart give no indication
of the pain hidden inside.

My heart is bleeding with a longing to see her.
It is just like a mirror
held by the henna-colored hands
of the intoxicated idol.

The fire could not do the harm
that my desire to slowly burn myself
did to me.
I have lived with so much sadness
that my heart got burned.

There is such allure in your image
that by virtue of hundred longings,
it has opened itself
like a rose to embrace you.

What is ringdove? A fistful of dust.
What is nightingale? A cage of colors.
O my lament, what is the mark
of an afflicted heart?

Your coolness
has tamed the wildness of my heart.
When you lack courage and
you are loved by someone,
the results are devastating.

When you have made a pledge
to stay in the prison of love,
your claim of fidelity
is like your hand
placed under a heavy stone.

You revealed the condition
of the martyrs of the past.
Your sword reflects images
like a mirror.

O the brightness of the sun,
turn to me as well.
Like a shadow, a strange time
has fallen on me.

I should get credit
for the sins not committed.
O God, it's a question of fairness.
Because I'm punished
for sins committed.

Ghalib, don't be disheartened
by the indifference
of the folks around you
because you have no one to call your own.
But there is God, dear me,
that you can always call your own.

A HIKE UP THE MOUNT SINAI

Your face was acceptable
to the splendor of eternal light.
It was only through you
that deeply held secrets of manifestation
were revealed.

In this blood stained shroud of your victims
there are millions of embellishments.
Enough to get the attention
of the fairies of the paradise.

O inhospitable preacher!
Neither you drink
nor you offer others.
What's so special
about your wine of paradise?

She is arguing with me
on the Day of Resurrection.
Why did I rise up from my grave?
Probably, she hasn't heard
the sound of the clarion.

The spring is coming and
that is why the nightingale
has started to sing.
And the garden birds
are spreading the rumor.

There are no idols in Kaaba
though they were once there.

Idols have thus some connection
with the holy place.

God doesn't give one and the same
answer to each questioner.
If in doubt, take a hike up the Mount Sinai
and know it for yourself.

There was nothing wrong
if she had an uncivil tongue.
There are limits, of course.
Eveyone I spoke to
was full of complaints.

Please take Ghalib
in this journey with you.
Whatever bounties I receive
from this pilgrimage,
I would humbly offer to
Your Majesty![66]

NOTORIOUSLY INFAMOUS

My weak heart can't take it anymore.
Some of this anguish is caused
by the paucity of red wine.

I'm embarrassed to tell Saqi
that there is too much sedimentation

66 The poet is requesting the Emperor who is getting ready to go on the Hajj pilgrimage.

in the red wine.
It shows my willingness
to accept anything.

There is no arrow in the bow.
There is no hunter near the bush.
Sitting in the corner of a cage
I'm pretty comfortable.

How can I believe that prayer
is free of hypocrisy?
There is too much greed
for the prayer to be only
for the sake of God.

Which particular path
the smart ones are following?
It is very common to follow the tradition
or copy the popular trend.

Let me stay at Zamzam.
What benefit am I going to get
going around Kaaba?
My garb is too much
drenched with wine.

It would be really sad if we can't make
things work between us.
You are not saying no to anything.
And I'm too persistent.

O the Angel of Death,
my liver hasn't liquefied
into a pool of blood

and it hasn't yet found
a channel to drip through my eyes.
You have to wait.
Let me live because there is so much
for me to finish.

Is there anyone
who doesn't know Ghalib?
He is a damn good poet
but notoriously infamous.

ONCE AGAIN

One again
  I want to play host to my beloved.
  Let the wine and goblets get so excited
  that they illuminate
  the place of our meeting.

Once again
  Let me collect the pieces of my liver.
  It has been quite a while
  that I offered a feast
  for her eyelashes.

Once again
  I'm afraid I have started to smother
  at the demands of staying sober.
  It has been years
  since I tore up my collar.

Once again
My breath is spewing
the fire of my laments.
It has been a long time since
I went to see a display of lamps.

Once again
the passion of my mad love
is inquiring the condition of my heart,
after it has already gathered
hundred thousand saltshakers.

Once again
I'm dipping my pen
in my heart's blood.
I want to draw some flowers
on the hem of my garment
to get her attention.

Once again
The heart and the eyes
have started their rivalry.
One is thinking about her,
and the other is looking at her.

Once again
My heart is taking me
to the valley of rebuke,
having demolished
the idol-temple of my pride
where I used to live.

Once again
The desire is looking for a buyer
to offer the merchandise
of wisdom, heart, and life.

Once again
My mind goes back
to tulips and roses
while embracing
a hundred thousand gardens
for the pleasure of my eyes.

Once again
I want to open the letter
from my beloved,
ready to sacrifice my life
at the heart-stealing envelope.

Once again
The desire wants me
to see someone
at the balcony,
with dark tresses
covering her face.

Once again
I want to confront someone
who has dagger-like eyelashes
sharpened by black antimony.

Once again
I want to see her charming,
spring-like fresh face,
flushed under the influence of wine.

Once again
My heart longs to settle myself
at someone's doorsteps,
mercifully pleading
with the doorkeeper.

Once again
My heart is searching for
days and nights
of carefree abandon.
Just sitting, doing nothing,
and thinking of her.

One again
Do not poke fun at Ghalib
because the flood of his tears
is ready to get loose.
He is sitting calmly but determined
to stir up a storm
if taken to the edge.

I'VE SUNG MANY SONGS

It is good news
that my heartless friend is cruel.
It leaves few options for Heavens
to dole out.

Her eyelashes
may be looking for some fresh blood.
I need to keep the blood of my eyelashes
for my own use as well.

O Khizr, we are the living ones
who know other people and the world.
Unlike you, we are not hiding like a thief
to claim an eternal life.

Even while living in misery
I knew people who were jealous of me.
Your charm and style, as others saw it,
was a calamity for my life.

O Heavens,
don't keep me away from her
because I'm not the only one left to be tested
by the long arm of the assassin.

I'm like a captive bird
who is collecting straw
to build a nest in the cage.

He thought that I was a beggar
and he ignored me.
I grabbed the feet of the gatekeeper
for letting me sit there
to get a glimpse of her.

Relative to what I want to say,
ghazal is not the medium
best suited to the vastness
of my poetic imagination.

God gave to the less fortunate as well
so that they don't cast an evil eye

on the gifts that Tajammal Hussain Khan[67]
received with His grace.

I don't know whose name
crossed my tongue, my God,
that the words that poured out
started to kiss and smooch my lips.

In the Emperor's reign,
the world is just too busy
beautifying things.
God will have to create more stars
to keep the sky illuminated.

The paper is finished
but the song to be sung
is not yet finished.
To travel across this ocean
of beautiful words
a new fleet is needed.

Ghalib, I've sung many songs
in my distinctive style.
The rest is for the critics
to turn over in their heads.

---

67 Nawab Tajammal Hussain Khan was one of Ghalib's benefactors. There is another couplet after this one that praises the Nawab. That couplet has not been translated.

A Chronology of Ghalib's Life Events

1797	Born December 27 in Akbarabad, near Agra
1810	Married Umrao Begum
1811	Moved to Delhi
1827	Traveled to Lucknow and Benares and then to Calcutta
1829	Returned to Delhi after 2 year stay in Calcutta
1837	Emperor Bahadur Shah Zafar ascends the Mughal throne
1841	The first edition of Urdu Divan is published
1845	The first edition of Persian Divan is published
1847	The second edition of Urdu Divan is published
1850	Emperor's tutor Muhammad Ibrahim Zauq dies
	Emperor honors Ghalib with two high sounding titles
1851	Emperor employs Ghalib to write a chronicle of Mughal Empire
1852	Ghalib's adopted son Arif dies
1855	Ghalib agrees to tutor Yusuf Ali Khan, Nawab of Rampur
1857	Ghalib's younger brother Yusuf Mirza Khan dies
	Emperor issues a decree supporting the Mutiny on May 12
	Emperor is arrested by the British forces on September 20
	Emperor's sons and a grandson shot dead in public view
	Emperor is exiled to Rangoon, Burma, after a show trial
1858	Ghalib publishes *Dastanmbo* in Persian on the events of 1857
1861	The third edition of Urdu Divan is published
1862	The fourth edition of Urdu Divan is published
	Emperor dies in exile
1863	The second edition of Persian Divan and the fifth edition of Urdu Divan published
1868	The first of several collections of Ghalib's letters published
1869	Ghalib dies February 15
1870	Umarao Begum passes away on her husband's first death anniversary

Further Reading

Ahmad, A. ed. 1994. *Ghazals of Ghalib: Versions from Urdu.* New Delhi: Oxford University Press.

Bly, R. and Dutta, S. 2001. *The Lightening Should Have Fallen on Ghalib.* Selected Poems of Ghalib. New Delhi: Rupa & Co.

Husain Y. 1977. *Urdu Ghazals of Ghalib.* New Delhi: Ghalib Institute Publishing.

Islam, K. and Russell, R. 1994. *Three Mughal Poets: Mir, Sauda, Mir Hasan.* New Delhi: Oxford University Press.

Kanda, K. C. 1977. *Urdu Ghazals: An Anthology.* New Delhi: Sterling Publishers.

Narang, Gopi Chand. 2013. *Ghalib's Thought, Dialectical Poetics & the Indian Mind* (Text in Urdu). New Delhi: Sahitya Akademi.

Newborn S. 1996. *Ghazals of Ghalib.* Santa Barbara, CA: Bandanna Books.

Niazi, S. K. 2002. *Love Sonnets of Ghalib.* New Delhi: Rupa & Co.

Parigarnaya, N. 1986. *Mirza Ghalib: A Creative Biography.* Karachi: Oxford University Press.

Russell R. and Islam, K. 2003. *Ghalib: Life, Letters and Ghazals.* New Delhi: Oxford University Press.

Sadulla, S. 1965. *Selected Verses of Mirza Ghalib.* London: Darwen Finlayson Ltd.

Saran, S. 1976. *Mirza Ghalib: The Poet of Poets.* New Delhi: Munshiram Manoharlal Publishers Ltd.

Schimmel, A. 1979. *A Dance of Sparks – Imagery of Fire in Ghalib's Poetry.* London: East-West Publications.

Varma, Pavan K. 1989. *Ghalib, The Man, The Times.* New Delhi: Penguin Books.

Acknowledgements

My commitment to life is best described by a quote from Taoist classic *Tao Te Ching*: "Be the valley of the universe so all things will come to you." Of the many gifts that life bestowed on me, the most precious was love of books and reading and for this I have to thank my father, Sardar Kandhar Singh Shaida, who was himself a poet and who introduced me to the Complete Works of Shakespeare and Divan-e-Ghalib before I entered high school. These books changed my life in significant ways.

Ghalib has been a companion—both his Divan as well as his poetry that reached me through vinyl records, cassette tapes, CDs, and digital downloads in the most melodious voices of our time–for a very long time. But one thing always frustrated me--how poorly the work of this great poet had been translated into English. I dreamed of changing this one day.

My initial translation of about 20 ghazals was seen by Ghalib scholar and highly acclaimed Urdu and English poet, Dr. Satyapal Anand, who encouraged me to continue with my quest. Thanks Dr. Anand for your encouragement.

The real turning point in this odyssey came when Dr. Gopi Chand Narang put his stamp of approval on my work. Dr. Narang is the greatest living literary critic of Urdu language and he has been rightly honored by the governments of India and Pakistan for his extraordinarily enriching contributions to Urdu language and literature. This much is well-known. But what is generally not known is the fact the he is also a Ghalib scholar of exceptional merit. His recent book on Ghalib has shed light on aspects of Ghalib's poetry that were previously unknown. When Dr. Narang gave the signal that I was on the right track I felt emboldened. Thank you Dr. Narang from the bottom of my heart.

I would like to thank distinguished academics, Dr. Shafey Kidwai from Aligarh Muslim University; Dr. Frances Pritchett from Columbia University; and Dr. Aamir Mufti from University of California, Los Angeles, for taking the time to read selections from the manuscript and for their very kind endorsements. This meant a lot to me.

I would like to thank Dr. Zafar Iqbal, President of GOPIO, Washington Chapter and Dr. Tahsin Siddiqi, University of Michigan, Ann Arbor, for their support.

The appeal of any book to the reader is not only the content or the subject matter but how it is packaged and presented. I would like to thank Joe Anderson, my publishing consultant at Partridge Publishing and his talented team for doing excellent work, from the cover design to the layout and for paying attention to the minutest details.

My wife and lifelong partner, Daler Aashna Deol, has always been a guiding light for me. My work on Ghalib came at a time when she was extremely busy with her TV program on "poets and poetry" in addition to working on two of her own poetry collections due for publication next year. Yet she was always there for me, to critique and to suggest improvements. Thanks, dear!

Our children, Raj and Rinku, and our grand children, Isha and Kieran, have not known Urdu language but they like good poetry and are pleased to know that in this book they have verse that they can access in the language that they understand. You are welcome, dear all!

A word for my readers: My sincere thanks to you for getting this book. I hope Ghalib's poetry in this translation will provide you with rich mental, emotional, and spiritual nourishment that I intended my readers to obtain. I would greatly appreciate your feedback. You can write to me at my email address: integralthinker@yahoo.com. You can also follow me on Twitter, Facebook, and my author website at Partridge.

Twitter	@surin_d
Facebook	facebook.com/surinder
Author Website	www.ghalibbydeol.com

CPSIA information can be obtained at www.ICGtesting.com
Printed in the USA
BVOW07s1955140714

359155BV00001B/7/P